PEANUT BUTTER *and* NAAN

Published 2014
Printed in the United States of America
ISBN: 978-1-63152-911-5
Library of Congress Control Number: 2014941650

Book design by Stacey Aaronson

For information, address:
She Writes Press
1563 Solano Ave #546
Berkeley, CA 94707

Peanut Butter

AND *Naan*

STORIES OF
AN AMERICAN MOM
IN THE FAR EAST

Jennifer Hillman-Magnuson

SHE WRITES PRESS

*F*or Bob,

without whom I wouldn't have adventures to write about, our beautiful children, or the knowledge of what unconditional love feels like. Thank you for growing with me through this life. I love you.

PROLOGUE

I'm an intrepid foreign correspondent just a few hundred miles from the Pakistan–India border. Picture Christiane Amanpour with better hair and no angry frown lines—but definitely with her ability to wear a scarf. I am precisely the kind of woman you wouldn't think twice about sending to the front lines to cover what will end up as the next CNN International headline. In fact, it's rather ridiculous how worldly I am, given how easily I also maintain my trademark, down-to-earth, approachable je ne sais quoi, which makes me an icon hailed the world over. Of course, I handle this heady mixture of fame and brilliant journalistic smarts in ways that make women want to be me (I have a scarf line coming out, due to my slightly superior method of jauntily knotting it just so) and men clamor to bed me. And yet somehow, *somehow*, I manage to stay refreshingly *me*.

I cross my toned, dancer-like legs and wonder if I should have left my Louboutins at the hotel and gone with a simple Prada bootie. Seriously, why didn't my stylist consider the sandy soil of northern India? Mental note: I need to hire Jennifer Aniston's people.

Thunk. The jolt of the car halts my reverie, and I rub my eyes, which have become dry from the dust-filled air. All that is left of my fantasy is that I really am nerve-rackingly close to Pakistan—although, oddly, I feel entirely relaxed. It's not something many blond American women raised on a steady diet of Hello Kitty, *Three's Company*, and roller skating to a ubiquitous inner soundtrack of tough-ass rocker chicks putting notches in their lipstick cases figure in their list of Calgon moments.

But I suppose you get any mother alone in a car without her children in any locale and tranquility is a foregone conclusion. In my case, as a breeder of five, I am practically channeling my inner Jeff Spicoli, I'm so peaced out. This comes as no real surprise to me, though, as I have openly fantasized about being so desperate for time alone that I've concluded prison might be a viable option for solitude. Pick a nonviolent crime (or, for the more daring, go ahead and mow down a known child predator with the minivan), and get guaranteed time *all alone* in which to read, exercise, and avoid bad prison food (and hence lose that last fifteen pounds). It's a great idea. If you are reading this from the relative privacy of your bathroom while some child pounds away on your door, demanding that you go feed him something, you're welcome.

Vigilante opportunities being scarce, my imagined halcyon days in a white-collar prison are easily swapped for the backseat of a questionably safe sedan somewhere on the outskirts of Delhi, bound for Agra. I am going to see the Taj Mahal with someone I hardly know these days—myself.

Our car hurtles past a semiarid landscape punctuated with splashes of red, gold, and fuchsia bougainvillea climbing implausibly over stone walls surrounded by dust and rocks. Peacocks perch themselves on boulders, sharing space with the cows, ducks, horses, chickens, and occasional monkey that make up the incredible roadside wildlife found in this region. Although I have spent a ridiculous amount of time in my own car as an amateur chauffeur (being paid only in sass, eye rolls, squirreled-away sippy cups containing coagulated glops of milk, and enough Goldfish to choke Shamu), I have not been behind the wheel of a vehicle for four months.

To drive in India is to narrowly escape death several times a day, so I force my attention out the side window. To do otherwise would ensure I would go mad with terror on this derelict, rut-filled road where workers were spared the labor of installing lane lines, since no one adheres to them anyway. We swerve to avoid an ox-drawn cart, and my lap strains against my seat belt as we briefly hurtle into the path of oncoming buses and trucks. Oddly, I do not clutch my armrest in a white-knuckled panic, contemplating my funeral and whether or not my husband will immediately remarry and whether or not I will haunt him for jumping into bed with some woman who is clearly insane because, *hello*, she'll inherit five kids along with my term life policy. Instead, I notice how the sunlight is filtered by the smoky haze produced by the tens of millions of people living in the city receding behind me, rendering everything mildly surreal. It's like looking through the world from behind a wedding veil, and I quite like it.

We whiz past towering white-stone temples with tinny Hindi music bleating from loudspeakers affixed to spindly turrets with a little wire and luck. It's such a contrast with the southern state of Tamil Nadu, where I live, and where temples sprout up between concrete buildings on every street in a riot of colors and faces and arms, every towering inch a jumbled mass of gods and goddesses. We wind through the village of Faridibad, whose aesthetics are more like those of my temporary Indian home with its piles of trash, water buffalo, and hogs alongside each other in the muck. Street dogs with long, sad-looking teats (which look disturbingly familiar and cause me to straighten up from my slouch) push tiredly at bright cans and boxes, unmindful of the potential slaughterhouse of cars just feet away. Either the animals are smarter in India or the scavengers are hungrier, since I never see roadkill.

Our driver announces that we have to take a detour, as he has just learned of an enormous traffic jam ahead. How he came about this knowledge is beyond me, since we are still moving and he has not spoken on a telephone. I imagine it must be from one of the many abbreviated conversations he held with pedestrians when we were crawling through various villages. He is a small man, more typical of drivers than the unusually burly former weightlifter we employ at home. After the first month, I got over the insecurity that comes from towering over men and knowing you outweigh most of them by at least twenty pounds. Of all the fears I feel in India, physical intimidation by a male isn't one of them—a little envy over their waist-to-hip ratio, yes. I notice his long, tapered nail beds and how the pinky nail on his left hand is longer than the others, though all need a serious trim. A nail gnawer myself, I have painstakingly grown out my own, so intent am I on not accidentally ingesting any type of pathogen.

When the driver alerts me to our detour, I find myself filled

with childlike excitement for an adventure. Onward! But then—
not surprisingly, this being India—the detour leads to a traffic
jam. And also not surprisingly, a diversion that would typically be
viewed in the United States as annoying at best or day-ruining at
worst instead contains small treasures along the way that we
wouldn't get if we were moving quickly. Our windows rolled
down, we pass street vendors selling savory *kachoris*; their aroma
of spiced lentils and vegetables in round pastries fried golden-
brown wafts toward our car in a beckoning finger of scent that
makes me swallow hard. We don't dare stop, though, since we
don't know how fresh they are; street food in India can be a
heavenly epicurean experience but, if not properly cooked, always
presents the lurking possibility of illness.

Eventually we slow down next to a man seated roadside,
roasting hot nuts, and our driver yells something through the
window. My fellow passenger (and closest friend in India) pushes
on my arm. "Quickly, hand him this." She thrusts five rupee coins
in my hands. I manage to toss them in the general vicinity of the
nut man, but our car is still inching forward, so I figure we've just
donated a few cents to some lucky vendor. But within moments,
he materializes alongside our car, clutching a brown sack in one
hand as he runs barefoot. Before I know it, he drops a steaming
bag on my lap and disappears as quickly as he came. The peanuts
are roasted in pans filled with red sand, and after I've spent ten
minutes greedily shelling nuts, my fingers are stained ocher. I look
like a bride fresh from her *mehndi* session, her henna-dipped
fingers signaling the nearing festivities.

I finish my snack with a fresh plum I brought with me from
the Kohn market in Delhi, and I have never felt more romantic or
decadent as the fruit's sweet-tartness fills my mouth. I lustily wipe

away juice from my chin and think in amazement that a typical on-the-go snack when I'm driving my minivan around in America usually consists of a Chick-fil-A and a Diet Dr. Pepper. I tell this to my friend, and she responds with her characteristic bluntness: "That is stupid. Just eat raisins or something from now on."

I love the way my friend, Shemain, talks. There is no pretense, no couching of phrases. We are nearly the same age, but we lack the trove of shared cultural references that can bond women within minutes of first meeting each other: *Hey, I'm Jen; nice to meet you. You also have a fifteen-year-old daughter? Do you love how we're now rendered idiotic? The other night, I heard my teenager listening to a remake of "Our Lips Are Sealed," and I tried telling her about my first Go-Go's album, and she kept looking at me like my brains were leaking out of my ear. I think she was trying to mask the fact that she didn't know what an album was, but whatever. We can talk at them all we want, but all she'll hear is "Muah muah muah," like Charlie Brown's teachers. Am I right? Let's go grab a Starbucks.*

It's almost like having a girlfriend from the evil Emperor Zurg's Planet Z (alas, a Disney/Pixar reference Shemain would not greet with familiarity and would thus dismiss as pedestrian), and I know she thinks the same of me.

Of course, the seed of human experience is the same when stripped of its cultural chaff, and after months of shared company, it hardly matters. Shemain is my friend, my landlord, and the sole person whom I consult on all things India. She has given up a chance to see her brother play in a polo match in New Delhi so that I can erase "See Taj Mahal in Person!" from my bucket list. So, at the mention of raisins, I nod my head and murmur, "Yeah, raisins are probably a better health choice than chicken breast fried in peanut oil and served on an oily white-bread bun." I can't help myself; I swallow hard again.

It's odd driving along like this on a Tuesday, heading to the world's most famous monument to love. I should be at a PTA meeting filled with overzealous volunteer moms who rabidly sink their teeth into the task of raising their children with a bloodlust fueled by latent bitterness over left-behind careers. I should be grudgingly agreeing to die-cut 74,000 pilgrim heads for the book fair and then snapping at my children about it—all in the name of being a good, involved parent. Instead, I have left all five of my kids in the care of my husband and several people who scarcely speak English on the Bay of Bengal, over a thousand miles to the south of me.

I have chosen to take my family as far from the land of shirtless Abercrombie models, drive-throughs, clean drinking water, and Target as I can. We are both literally and metaphorically a world away from our pampered American lives deep in the heart of a suburban bubble I semiendearingly refer to as the Beverly Hills of the South. I have a child experiencing her first year of high school without the social lubricant of Miss Me jeans and a new Dooney & Bourke bag, and a second grader who chose to be homeschooled rather than do yoga in PE class. My children have started to forget what breakfast cereal tastes like, they haven't seen a television commercial in over four months, and I buy my produce at a market as stocked with flies, cow feces, and naked children as it is with green beans.

The big question, I suppose, is why.

CHAPTER 1

"Ingrates!"

Some parents tenderly affix endearing nicknames to their offspring in a nod to their personality quirks or as a love language or maybe as an allusion to a favorite sport or activity. Some boys are Tiger, Sport, Boo Boo, or Big Guy. Perhaps your daughter is Angel, Princess, Baby Doll, or Pumpkin.

That's sweet. Really. In my husband's and my case, it was a toss-up between giving each kid a number ("Hey, you! Number Two! I'm not even kidding—if you punch Number Five one more time, you're in your room the rest of the night!") and assigning an all-inclusive name to the group. We went with the latter option, as we felt it had both a universal truth to it and also enough tongue in cheek–ness that our kids would know we had a sense of humor. Because we all know how important a sense of humor is when you decide to jump off the deep end and start making people.

It's not as if we are destined for a reality show. We don't have two dozen children or any multiples. We're not giants or dwarves. We're not even Kardashians. We do happen to have five kids, though, and these days that's still the kind of family that elicits unsolicited commentary from perfect strangers. It's stunning how someone in the checkout line feels perfectly comfortable asking me if I know how to prevent myself from becoming pregnant again. It's most certainly a testament to my self-control that I have never once told some meddlesome biddy in line at Walgreens that I have *no idea* how to stop them durn babies from comin'; all I knows is whenever my cousin and I play Hide the Corncob Pipe, I git a baby sooner or later.

So, yes—five kids. And although you never would have guessed it if you had met me or my husband back in college, we manage to support them all in a fairly elevated lifestyle. And I suppose it's that very lifestyle that's both the blessing and the curse that comes from the drive to give our own family the advantages and opportunities we never had growing up— although if you had asked me back in 1989 if I wanted five children, I would have spewed my forty-four-ounce Big Gulp all over my Levi's 501s and clutched my prescription for Ortho Novum a little too tightly. If you had told me I was going to marry the fraternity boy with the briefcase who gave me a life-insurance policy for our six-month anniversary, and that, after breeding five times, we would move to the Deep South and eventually to the third world, I would have told you to strap on your jet pack and hightail it back to your spaceship on Planet Crazy.

But obviously, things changed. We moved around for Bob's career as a health care executive and found that we liked it. And as each child was born, neither of us felt "done" until our fifth,

Henry, came along. I instantly fell in love with having young ones in the house. I find the innocence of early childhood intoxicating; if there is such a thing as an addiction to having babies, then sign me up for that twelve-step program. As an added bonus, I discovered that babies can be an extraspecial balm when you have older children morphing into teenagers. Nothing quite takes the sting out of snarling adolescent vitriol than the proffering of a sweet, chubby hand and a well-timed "Mama."

"Ingrates!"

I jabbed at the newspaper in my hand and gave my daughters and their two friends my most pointed look. They looked like models, with their long, shiny hair perfectly parted on the side and their fitted preppy sweaters with grosgrain ribbon. Their tight, size 00 jeans were stuffed into boots that always remind me of those horrible moon boots my generation once wore but cost a hell of a lot more. As hip as I had felt earlier in the day in my boot-cut jeans and swishy knit top from J.Crew, there is just no comparison when you're standing next to the effortless radiance that beautiful young girls give off.

They were seated at the counter, snacking on ramen noodles and doing what they did best: ignoring my pointed looks and my voice, and splattering broth over my newly polished granite countertops. I had just read an article about a young woman who had graduated from our local high school only a few years before. She had gone on a short mission trip with her mom to Uganda the summer before her freshman year in college. Only instead of going back home, going to college, dating the guy she'd likely marry, and settling down, she had stayed on. Not only that, she was now the adopted mother of fourteen orphaned girls from Uganda and spoke of a tale that involved God commanding her to do His will and work on Earth and take in these shattered children. And she had, all because God told her to do it.

My kids have a hard time obeying when I tell them to turn off their Xbox.

"Girls, seriously." I jabbed at the paper again. "I want to read this to you, and I want us all to be *inspired*." Frankly, I should have known better. If I wanted to grab their attention, I was better off telling them I had Justin Timberlake hog-tied naked on the dining room table, along with a sack full of cash for them to spend at the mall. Newspaper articles about young saints adopting babies aren't nearly as catchy with kids these days.

But they humored me, and, as my one-year-old clung to my leg like a spider monkey and my other two boys played their DS games from the family-room couch, I read a story to my children that would be the seedling for enormous personal growth in our family. I just didn't know it yet.

Although I was not lacking in dutiful grandmas who sent me storybook Bibles growing up, my knowledge of the Good Book is pretty limited. But there's a story I do know. It's the one about the flood, and how the waters washed away the old to prepare for the new. It's a story of cleansing and rebirth and forgiveness, and even those of us who don't know our Bible that well know the saga of Noah. A few days after I read this article to a marginally interested audience, our little suburb was submerged in Nashville's greatest flood on record. Over the course of one weekend, streets were transformed into rivers, cars were at the bottom of lakes that had only just been parking lots, and the local news ran clips of a forlorn house being swept away down I-65. People lost their homes and their belongings, and some even died.

As luck would have it, our house was perched atop a grassy hill, so, although we were stranded for a few days without a boat to take us to the store, we were let off relatively easily. In my gratitude for being spared, and with a houseful of restless kids whose schools were closed due to the waters, I decided we were going to give back and make a difference. We were going to get off our asses and be good people, dammit. When the water level reduced, we collected cans of food, shopped for blankets and flashlights and bottled water, and dropped it all off in the foyer of our church, which had become overrun with donations for flood victims.

There is obviously nothing wrong with buying things for charity. But after I'd dragged the kids around town for hours to Costco, Publix, and Walmart so we could gather provisions for faceless victims, it was more a case of my feeling snippy at a carload of tired, whiny kids not wanting to shop anymore than an exercise in philanthropy. None of them was old enough to go help tear down moldy walls in the homes devastated by floodwaters; most were too young to ladle out dinner in a soup kitchen; and we were up against a nice problem to have in a community: *everyone* wanted to help. The volunteer opportunities to aid the flood victims on the e-mail list we signed up for filled up before we had a chance to read about them, country-music stars held telethons to raise funds, and the nation rallied around our soggy Music City. So, though we continued to give money and food, I still felt a growing emptiness in my belly that wouldn't go away.

Before my sons were born, back when the girls were toddling around their Montessori preschool, I was a social worker. I worked in a DA's office in the felony-crimes unit, and my job paid just enough to cover student loans, groceries, and the delicious luxury of a once-weekly housekeeper who organized my dresser drawers and didn't balk when I nearly proposed marriage to her the first time I saw my neatly folded Hanes Her Ways. The job made up for my low salary with the kind of satisfaction that stems from helping people because you really want to. I could have been a business major—although that was highly unlikely, as I remember teasing my college roommate for her decision to major in computer science. My stinging rebukes were along the lines of, "Why would you major in computers? What do you do with that, figure out a better way to play Pac-Man something?" It was that lack of fiscal foresight that navigated me to an education in the liberal arts and a future career with long hours and less pay than my nanny currently earns.

It's also likely that another root of my academic and professional choices grew in the soil of a childhood that, while not exactly dysfunctional, held more than its fair share of quirks and ticks. On weekends when I was growing up, in Bend, Oregon, my parents and sister would be outside if the weather was nice, puttering in the garden or mowing the lawn or tending to any of the animals in our small coterie. My mom was belatedly going through her earth-mother phase (the '70s were at that point behind us), and while my friends at school feasted on lunches with such bounty as Dinty Moore pudding tins, Twinkies, and sandwiches made from Wonder Bread, I was subject to far more torturous fare. My Olivia Newton John lunch box reluctantly held a cargo of chewy brown-bread sandwiches that leaked watery homemade cheese (courtesy of our goat, Azalea). Ziploc bags contained a disappointing medley of homegrown sliced bell peppers, carrots, and cherry tomatoes, and the most excitement came in the form of a honey and carob–infused hockey puck of a cookie. My sister and I were allowed one glorious gift on the last day of school each year: a lunch containing anything we wanted. Anything. We. Wanted. Scores of nights had me lying in bed and clutching my Holly Hobby sheets as I endlessly shuffled through the various permutations—largely involving the Hostess food group—of what this most exalted of meals would contain.

As my family toiled away outside in an effort to grow more terrible things for me to unearth in the cafeteria, I stayed indoors and created a world over which I had total control. My favorite activity of all was vacuuming the dark brown shag in the family room. As the neat lines of the carpet fibers emerged from beneath the headlamp of our Electrolux, I imagined that the family room was a cruise ship and I was its captain. The sole mission of this vessel was to dock itself and gather the hobos from various ports and bring them back to the ship. That's where the magic happened. In addition to my seafaring skills, I was also gifted in the task of transforming these sad-sack street people into clean, attractive, productive members of society. I shaved, clothed, fed, and nurtured my passengers and then dropped them off at the next stop, ready to reenter society as erstwhile Liza Doolittles. Think The *Love Boat* meets *My Fair Lady*, and you're onto the kind of offbeat formative play that shaped at least part of who I am today.

The thing about helping people who are hurting and downtrodden and don't know what to do with their lives is that the payback is huge: you end up feeling really good about yourself. You tell yourself that the corporate schmucks who sold their souls to Intel and Microsoft (a shout-out to my college roomie on that one) don't have the *meaning* and soul-feeding goodness that your career path does. And you tell yourself that driving your kids to school in a rusted-out 1986 Saab during the year 2000 was part of what made you a better person. But let's be honest: even that starts to get old.

So when our procreating picked up and I got pregnant with our third, I quit working. And really, only so many years of volunteering at school, Girl Scouts, and the PTA can fill the space once taken up by holding a rape victim's hand or helping convict a man who chose to sleep with his daughter. For eight years I immersed myself in my kids the way I once had with my job. I helped out in their classrooms nearly every single day. I graded papers for overwrought teachers with a baby either in my belly or on my back. I baked cookies, muffins, cupcakes, and brownies for faculty appreciation. I iced, glittered, cut, and glued my way into being the perfect helicopter mom.

Meanwhile, with me at the helm of what bordered on manic familial nurturing, my husband's career flourished in ways we never expected. And while I have never been the most organized of women, I threw myself into the task of taking care of my family so Bob could focus on the job that would pay for our growing brood. One day we were young and struggling and I could barely afford extras like a magazine or a nice candle at the store, and then, as the years peeled away, we found ourselves with crow's feet and actual money in our checking account—*after the bills were paid.*

I tend to sugarcoat the past in my mind, and I have sometimes thought that if we could have just maintained our lives as they were at that exact point, we could have been more balanced. No debt, a little extra each month—a nice, normal life. Balance is something I have rarely had in my life, and it's been the greatest and worst thing about my personality. So when the career brass ring came within my husband's grasp and he took it, our lives became dizzyingly knocked out of equilibrium once more. Suddenly, we had money. We relocated away from our sleepy mountain town in the West and moved into an overly gilded McMansion (a house paid for by my husband's company) in a gated community just outside of Nashville, Tennessee. My painted foyer featured an Italianate mural that sprawled for twenty feet and made me uncomfortably aware of my old Costco couches. The vast, rolling lawns of Dolly Parton's estate sprawled directly across the street from our subdivision's gate, and rumor had it that when she was in a certain mood, a large bra would fly from the top of the wooden windmill that squatted on the front of her property.

I went from feeling like I was looking pretty snazzy when I showed up at the kids' schools in a new Eddie Bauer ensemble to being surrounded by women who were Botoxed, Juvédermed, bleached, and Juicy Coutured to within an inch of their lives. I pulled my trusty Dodge Caravan into my garage next to garages that housed NFL players' Lamborghinis, country singers' Hummers, and pampered housewives' Range Rovers. I had never been in this element before, and it intimidated, disgusted, and fascinated me all at once. And, being human, I was more than happy to finally afford a way to rid myself of those pesky crow's feet—and I always had a willing neighbor to guide me to the best Dr. Feelgood (or should I say Lookgood) in town. The first time I paid a ridiculous sum of money to a dermatologist to inject poison into my facial furrows, I looked into the mirror and felt a wave of exhilaration followed by a pang that I had crossed some kind of line. But that's an easy insight to sweep under the rug when your face doesn't match your age anymore.

At first it was heady, and we reveled in our new existence with gusto. We ate at the country club while a nanny watched the little ones, I shopped for clothes whenever I felt like it, and when we took the kids to Disney World, for the first time we didn't complain about the ten-dollar hot dogs and five-dollar sodas. But wherever you go, there you are, and I was still me. I held on to my clunky minivan and noticed a growing sadness blooming inside that no cute outfit or wrinkle-free face or charitable donation was going to fix. It was then, fresh on the heels of reading about that young woman in Uganda and our ill-fated attempts to assuage my abundance-driven guilt, that I drove myself to church and prayed harder than I ever had.

Dear God, hi. It's Jennifer Magnuson. I live at 75 Governors Way in Brentwood, Tennessee. Uh, Planet Earth. Anyway, I know I'm not the best about praying just to say thanks. So, first off, thank you. I know how great my life is and how it's actually pretty ironic that I call my kids the ingrates, because we both know that I'm not nearly as grateful as I should be, and I'm sorry. But that's part of why I'm contacting you. I need you to set me and my family on a path that will shake things up for us. I want us to do something really good and meaningful with our lives, and not just end up lazy and bored and pampered like so many people I've seen in my new neighborhood. I don't want to be bored! I want to be good, like that girl in the article I read. You know, the one with the fourteen adopted girls? I want to be like her! Well, kind of. Okay, I actually don't want to be that good. I really don't think I could handle another kid, much less fourteen. So let's say 20 percent as good as she is—which has still got to be pretty good, since she seems like a living saint. That should do it.

So anyway, I also need you to send me a really obvious sign that you've heard me if that's okay. You and I both know I'm not the best of your flock and I don't get to church nearly as much as I should—but hey, you created me, so don't get mad, okay? Okay. How about you send a pink car my way to show me you've heard me and are processing my request? Is that all right? I mean, how many people in this town drive a pink car? I don't think I've even seen one. Great. Okay, please bless my kids and my family and everyone else. Amen.

I understand that my heavenward communications aren't exactly what they teach you in Sunday school, but it is what it is. And the following Tuesday, as I sat at our cluttered dining room table, making the copious lists of what I would be doing for each kid during summer break, I got the call.

It was Bob, and he wanted to know how I felt about his perhaps accepting a temporary position in India, due to his company's new merger and blah blah blah de blah (I have trouble focusing when he gets into the excruciating business minutiae leading up to what he has to impart to me). He assured me it likely wasn't going to happen, but he needed my green light if he was to be considered for it. To which I blithely answered, *Sure! Of course! Should adventure come our way, who are we to turn it down? History favors the bold!*—all the while adding *register girls for dance camp* to page two of my list.

Later that afternoon, as I was racing around town, running my usual slew of errands, I chatted on my cell phone while parked at a red light. As I gabbed with my friend, I noticed a car pulling out of the gas station to my right. The phone fell from my hands and thunked to the floor of my car as my mouth also fell open. I felt a tickle in my belly as I watched a hot-pink Mustang convertible slowly pull out directly in front of me. And Scout's honor, by the time I had recovered my phone from the floor, Bob was beeping in. I clicked over.

"Jen. It's a done deal. We're going to India in six weeks. You might want to amend your lists."

Imagine, if you will, someone from India who has never been to the United States attempting to tell her kids they're about to move to America. Imagine that this person has also very limited, egregiously dated information about our country, and what she says to her kids will shape how they view this country until they get there. Some poor kid has been fed a bunch of cockamamie about how every man is a cowboy, the women are all Connie Sellecca, and there are solid-gold Rubik's Cubes in every Cadillac. So you see my quandary as I imparted the anemic contents of my India database to the kids, culled largely from "Rikki-Tikki-Tavi" and my brief foray into yoga in 1998, all of which serve to underscore not only my complete lack of world studies in my academic career but also my rather pathetic attachment to the '80s.

Come, children! Let me mollify your fears about moving across the world by saying that I think this grand adventure will be incredibly enriching for reasons yet unknown to us. We get to leave our comfort zone and, uh, see elephants! And Bollywood! And—ooh, let's see—bindis, *Slumdog Millionaire*, naan bread, curry, tigers, *The Jungle Book*, and cobras! But no, no, sweetheart, don't cry. Seriously, the cobras won't kill you. Yes, I know what your snake book says about them. Why won't they kill us? Because we're Americans, honey.

HOW TO APPLY FOR PASSPORTS FOR SEVEN
PEOPLE IN EIGHT EASY STEPS

1. Order original, sealed copies of several of the kids' birth certificates. Wonder why the only ones we have are coffee-stained copies of copies. Flog self for not being the kind of mom who has a hanging file folder labeled CHILDREN'S ORIGINAL BIRTH CERTIFICATES. Further flog self for not owning hanging file folders for anything. Kick wicker Christmas basket from 1997 that serves as file cabinet.

2. Wait for copies. Resend order once, as signature you uploaded to computer form does not match signature on scanned copy of driver's license and your order has been rejected. Obsess for the rest of the day about whether having inconsistent signatures is a sign of being crazy.

3. Get birth certificates in mail! Create folder for children's passports with certificates, forms, and Social Security cards. Feel full of self, knowing you're well on your way to becoming that organized file-folder mom, and celebrate with glass of wine. Spill some on folder. Resume flogging while practicing signature.

4. Schedule time for husband to meet you and kids at post office in Nashville. Get really excited on day you go, and manage to shower, dress, and get all five of the kids ready and in the car in less than three hours. This is really happening! Envision trip to Taj Mahal and matching pink and orange silk scarves you'll wear with daughters. Get stuck on highway for additional hour due to Country Music Association festival and subsequent additional eight hundred thousand tourists in

area for the week. Listen as kids' bickering escalates; attempt to lighten the mood, only to have your efforts met by surly teens' eye rolling. Mentally take back scarves. Plan on spending extra money on gold earrings for self.

5. Arrive at post office. Realize you have filled out wrong forms; fill out seven new ones while one-year-old teeters on your hip. Keep three-year-old from throwing all Priority Mail envelopes onto floor, and whisper threats of dismemberment to bickering older children, all the while keeping a fake smile plastered on face. Endure husband's anxious pacing as he fields numerous calls, texts, and e-mails on his BlackBerry. Remind him that you didn't make up the rule that states both parents have to be present to procure children's passports. Mentally upgrade earrings to diamonds and wonder if the Taj Mahal has a nice gift shop.

6. Successfully take passport pictures of four older children.

7. Attempt to have picture of one-year-old taken. Have terse postal employee explain that a tomato-faced, squalling baby gripping your chest isn't gonna fly for the passport people. Get creative by holding baby under arms and raising him above head, *Lion King*–like, while kneeling on floor of post office, facing white backdrop. When that only induces more screams, sit on stool, completely cover self in white sheet, and attempt to hold clearly terrified baby, who is now choking on tears and convulsing, no doubt because of strange ghost chair grabbing him and whispering into his ear to "sit on Mama's lap." Have husband run out to van for car seat; drape it in white sheet, only to see baby hiccup briefly and then resume screaming as soon as postal employee shows up with camera.

Have camera shoved into your hands by said employee as she mutters, "You try," and attempt to line up face of baby in precise crosshairs of camera lens as he hurls himself out of car seat and crawls madly away while a gathering crowd in post office wonders what the hell you have done to the child. Ask children to help pin baby's legs down in car seat as you remember he loves "The Wheels on the Bus." Disregard imagery of a deranged, Von Trapp–esque family and instruct everyone to break into song. As baby finally stops squalling, snap an acceptable picture.

Have picture of self taken. Try not to cry as you see the frazzle-haired, perspiration-soaked image and figure that's probably what you'll look like after each flight anyway. Sign forms with husband; swear oaths over documents as baby crawls away. Instruct eight-year-old to fetch baby and watch without caring one bit as he retrieves baby by ankles and drags him on his stomach across filthy marble floor of post office. Do not make eye contact with patrons as you mumble, "Don't drag your brother." Mentally upgrade carat weight of earrings.

CHAPTER 2

W hen I told my friends what we were planning on doing, and that we would be doing it in just a few weeks, they largely viewed me as a crazy woman. I think it's accurate to say that while a wise person looks before she leaps, I tend to leap first and scream, "Oh, shit!" mid-jump but keep leaping anyway. You just never know what will be there when you land.

Every day one of my girlfriends would call and beg me to reconsider taking five children to a third-world country. I got texts at all hours with links to articles on malaria, dysentery, typhoid, cholera, and terrorism, not to mention a lot of blank stares when I told teachers about our pending absence for the next four to six months. My mother, a woman possessing a sense of humor drier than a good wine, just chuckled when she got word of our plans. I know she worried, but she has been worried since I left the house for college. No matter how far-fetched my adventures have seemed to her, she has always supported me unconditionally while patting herself on the back that she was smart enough to have only two kids and be done with it. My neighbors didn't know what to do with me. Either I was the bravest woman on the planet, an exotic explorer off to live her own private *National Geographic* special, or they were reduced to the insight that India was "just so dirty" and asked was I at least going to bring along a case of hand sanitizer?

This is not to say that I didn't have a small cadre of supporters. A few of my more adventurous friends gave me the metaphorical thumbs up. Because I truly wanted to do it, I latched onto the positive feedback—as sparse as it was—and let that serve as my justification for the adventure I was certain would change our lives for the better.

And though I felt in my gut that this was where the universe wanted my family, that this leap of faith was our destiny, I can't say I knew exactly why. I suppose I imagined it would all sort itself out when we got there, and I made another mental note to ask God to be nice and specific and point it out for us. Because as much as I doubt myself, I admit I still believe in the signs I receive from the unseen—whether it's God, the universe, a guardian angel, or maybe just my dead grandma yelling at me from the afterlife to slow the hell down.

I didn't tell anyone about the pink car, because living in the Bible Belt has taught me that you do not impart any skepticism or unconventional thoughts about the man upstairs to your neighbors while living south of the Mason-Dixon Line; if you do, you run the risk of people's feeling for the horns on your head, or at least talking about you behind your back later. You know such gossip is imminent when a Southern woman sounds the death knell "Bless your heart"—code in the South for "You Yankee heathen thing, I cannot possibly let you into my bunko group with those strange liberal ways of yours. Now go—shave your underarms or kill a chicken for your statue of Hillary Clinton or whatever you people from out West do."

When pressed to reveal my motivation for taking five innocent kids out of their comfort zone and into the great unknown, for the most part I told these concerned souls we had to do it for my husband's job, and that I had prayed about it. The one critical aphorism I failed to consider was to be careful of what you ask for. If I learned anything during my year of preparation, it was this: *someone* hears us loud and clear and answers our prayers. And if that someone is God, I can attest to the fact that even heathens like me are heard. I'm not an atheist—I just have a mindset that pretty much anything could be "the answer" when it comes to faith and what happens when we die. My family sometimes goes to church, but it's usually to appease my in-laws or to satisfy my need to see my children clean and dressed up all at the same time.

Bob and I have encouraged our children to seek their own spiritual path and as a result have a house filled with agnostics, Catholics, humanists, and one Muslim. In my case, God heard me, held me to my word that I wanted to "shake things up," and wrapped up my request with a series of typhoid shots.

So take heed. Let the following stories of life in India with a large American family inspire you to get real specific with your own prayer request. At the very least, as someone once told me, I am an excellent person to use as an example of what *not* to do (thanks, Mom).

Because I have gone against the grain of my WASP heritage—multiple moves, more than 1.5 children, and a liberal outlook bordering on what some people call "woo-woo," I have always taken care to try to present my family to the outside world as a little less crazy than we really are, even though my home might be filled with frenetic activity, lost homework, and an abundance of colorful language. Still, as much as I try to impress people with how together our household is—and yes, I am well aware that many American women have an almost pathological desire to come off as a tear sheet from a Pottery Barn catalog—more often than not, I end up looking like a living public service announcement for birth control.

PSA, take one:

Hi. I'm Jamie Lynn Spears (or Bristol Palin, or any of the cast of MTV's *Teen Mom*—take your pick). *As spokesperson for Just Say No to Teen Pregnancy, I'd like to introduce you to our newest team member, Jennifer Magnuson. She's here as a part of the campaign to Stop Doing Too Much and Overloading Your Life in an Effort to Attain Spiritual Enlightenment When Really You Should Just Be at Your Kid's Soccer Game Like Everyone Else. Unfortunately, Jennifer can't actually be here, as she is trying to get seven people out of the United States before the Fourth of July and also fears she may have left one of her children at the local Waffle House while she was looking for her checklists under the bench seat of her minivan. Seriously, y'all, I just scheduled my tubal.*

I realize that the above announcement never happened, friends. But when you have five children, where else do you go for a respite but inside your own head? If the timing had been a little different, I would say Walter Mitty used *my* escapist techniques. Have you ever seen the movie *Home Alone*? It came out when I was a young adult, sometime during that sanguine period before children and marriage. I didn't have any real reason to see it, since I was probably too busy having sex, or sleeping in, or peeing by myself, or whatever else I did before domestic life lassoed me. But for some reason I did (to show my maternal side to some guy? Which would have led to more sex, sleeping in, and solo urinating), and I remember how one scene in particular from that movie stood out at the time. No, not the overplayed aftershave-on-the-cheeks bit, followed by the marginally funny–turned–ridiculously famous prolonged scream. I'm talking about the scene where Macaulay Culkin's huge family races through the airport—kids everywhere, bags flapping, parents panting while clutching their plane tickets—only to barely make their flight to Paris. The mom and dad have panicked expressions on their sweaty brows, and it's no surprise that people this harried managed to actually leave a child home alone. Limbs akimbo, helter-skelter, all those kids trying their best to keep up with the adults as the flight attendants shoo them into the loading dock of the waiting plane, they are a living advertisement for China's one-child policy.

My reaction back then was along the lines of, *Oh, come on. Who is that disorganized? Who has that many freaking children? Who would travel overseas with a posse of snot-nosed kids who don't appreciate that kind of thing anyway? Thank God that will never be me, as I am far too organized to let this kind of chaos become my life. Now, more sex, please.*

That was us, only our luggage wasn't nearly as nice as the stuff they had in the movie.

You can't fly direct to Chennai from Tennessee, so we ended up in Brussels for an extended layover. Brussels happens to be one of those charming, pristine European towns where most activities cater to adults. If you enjoy marveling at exquisite architecture, absorbing rich cultural history, smoking a lot of cigarettes, wearing well-made clothes, dining out, and window shopping at toy stores filled with intricately hand-carved boats that children may not actually touch, by all means, this is the place for you.

Take your grown-up self and revel in the lack of wailing babies in the cafés, the distinct absence of theme parks, and the void of beleaguered mothers chasing after errant toddlers in the park and waving leaky sippy cups in the kids' faces as they cajole them to just please stop drinking from the puddles. Imagine leisurely relieving yourself in a public restroom without having to try to simultaneously change a pull-up and not drop the other child before giving up, figuring that toilet water in Europe is probably almost as clean as tap water.

I didn't enjoy Brussels nearly as much as I thought I would.

Our foray into Belgium can be summed up with a visual of children sacked out on the hotel bed like a pile of milk-drunk puppies. The few pictures I managed to take of our family feature exhausted, surly-looking kids slumped in front of some shop on the Grand Place. My advice is this: if you ever need to move across the world with children whose bottoms you still wipe, just burn whatever money you have in your wallet and try to find a direct flight.

The icing on the *gaufre* came when we arrived at the Brussels International Airport only to be told it had no record of our connecting flight to India. Nothing—not even our names. Mind you, our tickets had been booked through Bob's company weeks before, and we had somehow managed to leave New York City and cross the Atlantic with ease. But here, we were just some crazy family, accompanied by the contents of a double-wide, knocking down the roped access to business class.

I would like to tell you that we handled this bump in the road with grace, but maneuvering that many people and belongings on strict timelines among people who speak another language—and in fact can't contain their sneer when you fumble with your recall of college French—brings out the worst in some of us.

I found myself slumped on one of our suitcases, holding a sleeping baby and trying not to lose sight of the other kids, who were wired from a breakfast of *café au lait* and *pain au chocolat*. When they told us there were no more direct flights to India with seven open seats for two days, I openly wept at the prospect of having to reload the mountain of travel gear back into three different cabs and rent another set of hotel rooms. I mean it—I actually sat there and cried like a baby. I'm sure Bob would have consoled me, but he was acting like an actual grown-up and dealing with the situation. Times like this make me realize how lucky I am to have the yin to my yang.

Of course, we could fly the next day to Bombay and take an eleven-hour train ride to Chennai, but the mere mention of that option induced only more tears. I knew they were motivated to help get us out of the country, if only to prevent us from putting a further damper on the tourism industry. I had thought I was doing things right by giving us a good four-hour window to get to the airport and on the plane in plenty of time to avoid boarding late and enduring the shell-shocked stares of passengers, who would inevitably mouth, *Please don't let them sit in my row. Please, God, not next to the baby*—but it was all for nothing.

Then, in a stroke of luck involving a delayed flight from Paris, the young man behind the Jet Airways counter (who spoke Dutch, as opposed to French, and was not snooty in the slightest), managed to find seven separate seats on the flight to India that was leaving the terminal in sixteen minutes.

We had less than twenty minutes to get through customs, clear security, and arrive at terminal B-48, at the farthest possible end of the airport—the amount of time it generally took our thirteen-year-old to decide on which ripped sweats to wear. Which explains how, one fateful day in July, many travelers at the Brussels International Airport believed they were at one point in danger of being trampled by a herd of wild bison. People actually clutched their boarding passes to their chests as we barreled past them.

I'm not proud of how we managed to get on the plane. How could we have appeared as anything different from what we were in that moment—a frantic mother and father barking orders at a small mob of children, all of us sporting matching I LOVE NEW YORK T-shirts? I was exactly what I didn't want to be: the ugly American traveler, a wild-eyed drill sergeant yelling at my family to get their things off the security conveyor belt and run as fast as they could. There wasn't even time to put our shoes back on.

We were a flurry of swinging diaper bags, superhero-emblazoned backpacks, and car seats. I held a pair of shoes in one hand and steered a stroller with the other as I hollered over my shoulder to the children wheezing behind me, "Let's *move*! There is *no* time! Girls, I told you to grab your bags and *run* as soon as we cleared security. I don't *care* if your feet hurt; we are going to miss this plane. Bob, do you have the passports? You *think* so? Who are you? One of our kids?

"My God, Jacob, you almost ran into that man—say you're sorry. Excuse us. Pardon me. Coming through. Woman with a baby. *People*, we are going to miss our plane—move the hell out of the way, *s'il vous plaît*! Run, dammit, *run*!"

So began our less-than-auspicious journey to India, a land celebrated for its spiritual mysticism, meditation, yoga, and movies that feature Julia Roberts caressing baby elephants after life-altering hours spent in an ashram. A land about to be invaded by seven Americans who for years hadn't gone more than a week without guffawing over an episode of *SpongeBob*.

Just how did I think this trip would transform my own family? If I give it serious thought, the thrill of becoming someone else, of slipping into some kind of *other*, has always held me in its grasp.

When I was eight, I bonded briefly with Kathie Marthaller, a glamorous redhead who led a dashing life far more adventurous than the middle-class drudgery I was saddled with. Kathie's mom shocked her family when she just up and left one day, leaving her carpenter husband behind to raise three children. This unexpected arrangement resulted in the dizzying riches and privileges that come with single parenthood: McDonald's for dinner at least twice a week, endless television viewing, and that most coveted of talismans that announces the hallowed status of latchkey kid—a house key on a bright blue piece of yarn around Kathie's neck. Kathie possessed the ability to *let herself into an empty house*. The key whispered seductively of her weekdays after school, alone hour after hour, cooking for herself and maturely answering the telephone. She was the luckiest girl I knew.

Before my mom got wind of the fact that adult supervision was in short supply at the Marthaller home (a mere nuisance, really), I was able to escape the slog of supervised playdates. For a few shining weeks, Kathie and I prepared our own snacks: melted hunks of cheese over crackers, all brazenly cooked under the broiler coils of a real oven. We used sharp steak knives to spread our peanut butter, simply because we could. We scanned the cable channels for *Porky's* and *Blue Lagoon*. We ordered her kid brother around or sometimes locked him out of the house for fun.

We played for hours with the contents of an ancient trunk with thick leather straps and a brass lock that had long ago been jimmied open. Kathy's mom had once been a hairdresser, and the trunk spilled over with booty: pink spongy rollers, expired perm kits, and, best of all, androgynous Styrofoam heads sporting wigs of every kind. Suddenly I wasn't Jenny, unfortunate owner of the Dorothy Hamill hairstyle that was incongruously paired with a love of Jessica McClintock calico prairie skirts; I was a foxy mama with a tight cap of raven-hued curls. Or someone exotic, usually named Alexandra, with a mane of perfectly frosted hair.

The same excitement I got from imagining a new start as a child still lives in me today. We move around a lot more than the average family, and it isn't always fun. But the thing that sustains my energy and excitement levels as I once again pack up the cookbooks alongside the Barbies and Hot Wheels is the opportunity to start fresh in the next community. Boise was the city where I wouldn't be the disorganized mom whose kids regularly wore mismatched socks to school. Flagstaff was where I would purchase and maintain a set of Tupperware containers and never end up with four warped plastic lids for every two bowls. In Vancouver, I would greet my kids after school with a snack I had thought out days earlier as part of my weekly meal planning. These are the coping mechanisms of people who move frequently for their career.

India would be the perfect place to shed our American skins, even if just for a while. We could press pause on our fumbling ways and find some much-needed direction for meaning and purpose. Surely, even the simple act of filling our lungs with foreign air would be an impetus for change! Inhale the new and exhale the old—the one who had been meaning to maintain a datebook of everyone's birthdays for ten years now.

Our plane touches down in Chennai just after midnight. We are about to be residents of the state of Tamil Nadu—formerly the city of Madras, a locale on the southeast corner of India, bordering the Bay of Bengal. Enormous by American standards, Tamil Nadu has roughly five million inhabitants, yet its size pales in comparison to the masses packed into the Delhi/New Delhi metro area: more than twenty-four million. India has more than one billion residents, and yet is physically less than one-third the size of America. This means there are no Montanas or Wyomings to offset the urban hubs. It is a teeming mass of flesh and blood and breathing things, every square inch occupied by something.

We stand in line for an interminable amount of time under the buzzing fluorescents of the small airport as customs officers inspect our passports and visas, question us on our stay, and scrutinize my children, who are at this point insane with fatigue. Mere feet away, outside the airport, hundreds of people mill about.

This is it. We are here! We are really here. The Chennai airport does not have skycaps to help with our multitude of bags, and if you are fortunate enough to have a driver or any kind of help, that person is not allowed inside the airport without a plane ticket, so you are on your own until you cross the threshold into the outdoors. We end up piling the younger ones onto the roller suitcases and roll our way out of the airport burdened like pack mules, only to take a refreshing breath of air as murky and stagnant as a Turkish steam bath. Though our most recent home, Tennessee, is known for humid summers that can peel off makeup within five minutes, this invisible wall of heat and moisture is unlike anything I have ever experienced. It is like trying to breathe through a wet washcloth. It instantly saps you of any energy, which in our case is especially low after flying across the globe with our kids—and makes the slightest task feel Herculean.

We scan the faces in the crowd for the drivers Bob's company has sent and immediately realize that most of the brown eyes in the throng are focused on us. Chennai doesn't have as many foreigners as other cities in India, such as Delhi, Bombay, Mumbai, or even Bangalore. This initial awareness that we are something of a spectacle will become ever-present for us wherever we go in the state of Tamil Nadu. Our kids will be touched, cheeks will be pinched, hair will be caressed, and pictures of my flaxen-haired daughters will be snapped constantly.

As we blink like newly foaled horses in the late-evening air, people crowd around ninane, ten deep. The cacophony of voices in myriad languages mixes with the honking of horns, the smell of gasoline, the whir and putter of auto rickshaws, and the groans and bellows of livestock. It's coming at us from all angles. The entire time I am in India, I will never feel as if I can truly escape her noises and smells, not even in the sanctuary of my own bed, so this is a proper introduction.

We finally spot our drivers, each carrying a hand-lettered sign that reads MAGNUSSON PEOPLE USA. Bob and I split up with the kids and pile into three cabs that remind me of the squat, steel, Soviet-era Studebakers from grainy old movies. I'm thankful we aren't in one of the yellow-and-black auto rickshaws that teeter along. They are equipped with three wheels, all smaller than those of an average tricycle, and lack doors or protective barriers of any kind. Many of them have cracked red rubber horns taped to their roofs; these are regularly squeezed, their puny squeaks announcing the rickshaws' presence on roads congested with cars, bicycles, animals, and people—and this is the traffic at one in the morning.

As my children sleep with their faces pressed against the car windows, spent from the thirteen-hour journey, our convoy of cars sputters past fruit stands piled high with pyramids of lychee fruit and pomegranates. Street vendors taking advantage of the nocturnal business generated by the airport crank heavy wrought iron handles, feeding stalks of sugarcane into a press that spits out a sugary juice called *rhuse*, which is popular throughout the country.

We drive along a seemingly endless stone wall that is punctuated every twenty meters or so with the beautiful, picturesque script that characterizes Hindi. What could it possibly say? *Welcome to India*? *We pray more than you*? It is so foreign! So terribly exotic! I beg my driver to translate the flowery prose that adorns the ancient-looking structure. He scarcely hesitates before informing me, "It says to please, no urinating here."

We plan on spending the next few days house hunting; our

rooms at the Taj Coromandel Hotel are booked and waiting for us. India is nothing without her celebrations, customs, and ceremonies, and even though it is now the early hours of the morning, we are greeted by a sight that I will always remember:

A beautiful young Indian woman in a striking teal-and-gold sari stands at the entrance of the hotel to welcome our family. Her shiny blue-black hair is tightly wound behind her neck and topped with a fragrant bloom of jasmine petals. In her outstretched hands is a round brass tray inlaid with the whorls and symmetrical designs I will come to associate with the Indian aesthetic. On the tray, a single lotus flower floats in an earthenware bowl, along with a small brass lamp releasing a flickering flame, and next to it an even smaller bowl—like a salt cellar—holds a neat little mound of red powder, called *kukumam*, which the woman ceremoniously applies to the spot on our foreheads right between our eyes, leaving us with the mark of *tilaka*.

We manage to put the kids to bed by the respectable hour of four, and fingers of sunlight are already peeking through the night's darkness before Bob and I go to sleep. I'm sure we could have collapsed earlier, but just after we get the kids down, we are increasingly disconcerted by the constant booms and cracks thundering just outside our hotel window, and I have Bob call our concierge.

I'm frightened, of course, and in my fatigue and culture shock have anxiously conjured a scenario wherein rebel forces are just outside our room, waiting to capture the newly arrived American family and take us to some spider-infested jungle to await their ransom payment.

"This is Bob Magnuson. For God's sake, it sounds like Beirut, Lebanon, outside. What on earth is going on? Oh. Yes, I see.

Okay, thank you. No, no. Good night." He hangs up the phone and gives me a sheepish look.

"Well, apparently it's Saturday, and that's when Indians get married. All the wedding halls in the city are still letting off fireworks and crackers for the celebrations. I guess this is a pretty regular thing."

I finger the grainy red dot on my forehead as I try to will sleep to come.

Welcome to India, Jennifer.

CHAPTER 3

Nawab Habibullah Avenue in the Nungambakkam district of Chennai is a clean, palm-lined street centrally located amid the bustling hub of the city. Like a thirteen-year-old in front of her mirror with a hairbrush microphone, I practice saying my street and neighborhood name until it flows off my tongue. *Nah wob hobby boola avenue in none gum bockun.* It doesn't take much to make me feel glamorous, and my ability to tell rickshaw drivers where I live gives me an inordinate sense of worldliness. Small victories like this buoy me, each one propelling me to the next—as well as making excellent playback fodder for my inner soundtrack to my hidden cool-girl persona.

We live inside a small, walled compound in a modest two-story stucco home. Even the whitewashed walls seem exotic to me, covered as they are in brightly colored flowers that never cease their blooming. Waxy pink and white frangipani flank the oxidized iron gate that marks the entrance to our courtyard, where we have just enough room to park our small rented minivan. Where another car might park sits a large backup generator that provides reprieve from daily brownouts. Our new place is appropriately named Frangi House, and a small ceramic nameplate wired to the mossy-hued metal verifies this for our visitors.

The street is a small oasis, really. We are lucky to find such a home, even if it means living among mostly Muslims and just one or two Indian families. Here, we are the foreigners, and we are reminded of our displaced status five times a day when one of the nearby mosques blasts the call to prayer. After the first few days, when I am finally convinced that I can't hear "jihad" or "death to foreign infidels" during it, I relax and learn to tune it out.

Most Western expats in Chennai choose to live along the Bay of Bengal in an enclave just off East Coast Road, infamous for the fact that one heavy rain can pit the road with sinkholes that are rumored to swallow people up. Rents are cheaper there, and the North Americans, Europeans, and Asians in India on corporate work visas live in large villas with swimming pools and gardens. They are also close to the arterial road that leads directly to the American International School, where Bob's and my oldest daughter, Maddie, is a student; I'm envious of this proximity because even with our skilled driver, Narynaan, whose last job was driving test cars for Ford in New Delhi, we have at least a forty-minute journey each way.

East Coast Road is also peppered with stores that cater to the Western palate. It's where you can buy leavened bread, jams, and even beef at outrageously inflated prices. I caved in to my desire for dairy at one point and pay over 2,500 rupees for the privilege of using suspiciously old cheddar for my grilled cheese. That's $60 for a sandwich you have to cook in a wok greased with buffalo ghee.

It also becomes quite apparent that Chennai isn't known for being the cleanest or most livable city in India. By Western standards, it's obvious that most of this country, in fact, falls woefully short in the sanitation department. But then, that's not why people are drawn here. Brochures for India boast of its mystical, vibrant, and enchanting qualities, not of its easy living. If we wanted to be in the land of hand sanitizer, squeaky-clean stores, and meat that comes packaged in plastic that belies the truth that it was recently a warm, breathing animal, I suppose we should have stayed in the suburbs.

Something tells me, though, that the answers I'm seeking don't exist on the racks at Ann Taylor or at the bottom of a Starbucks coffee (venti half-caf nonfat latte, no whip, one pump). So it's here, in the land of dirty enlightenment, that I find myself sipping my chicory coffee, which is already staining my teeth— and I don't care, because it runs circles around anything I've ever been given by some hipster barista—and wondering if my mom was right about my being a closeted adventure junkie. That, and exactly how long it will be before one of us succumbs to some tropical disease—a karmic retribution of sorts for not being the sort of mom who creates a gentle consistency for her children within the confines of one house at the end of a quiet cul-de-sac from which we never move.

And boy, have we moved. India is a startling mix of contradictions. The flowers and the jeweled hues of the saris, the tranquility of the yoga ashrams, and the savory smells that rise from the outdoor food stalls all commingle with the menagerie of animals that roam freely throughout traffic, people who think nothing of defecating in the streets, and slum after slum after heartbreaking slum.

Nine million people coexist in this Indian city on the southeast coast. Chennai, formerly known as Madras, is the textile capital of India and home to the noxious plaid of the same name worn exclusively by Hamptonites, golfers, and Ralph Lauren models. I get a kick out of wondering how many upwardly mobile preppies back in the States realize that their Brooks Brothers summer madras plaid pants are essentially ethnic wear.

We are tucked on the Bay of Bengal, although it takes us nearly an hour to drive from our home to the sea. The tsunami of 2004 taught a harsh lesson to those living too close to the water, and even today, the infrastructure of Chennai can scarcely handle a strong cyclone, much less the walloping devastation of a tropical storm or hurricane.

A heavy rain is enough to flood the streets, most of which are ill equipped—if at all—to cope with excess water. The frequent and unfortunate result of too much precipitation is a standing, murky mess that teems with waste and disease. Yet even in the midst of a tepid, mosquito-infested street, all I have to do to feel a spark of magic is raise my head and take in the outline of the trees against the sky. India is full of surprises, and for all her chaos, it is nearly impossible to impose my will and Western paradigm on this land. To survive here is to submit to the flow of each day—a lesson that is thrust upon me time after time during our entire stay in India and one that I fight until the end.

I never said I was a quick learner.

CHAPTER 4

I was told that nothing would prepare me for India until I got here. It's true—it's an incomparable place where almost every aspect of life is different from that of the West. No matter what you need done or when or where you need it, more likely than not, it will happen in "five minutes"—which, I quickly learn, can mean anything from immediately to two weeks from now.

Time in India has a fluidity that is a vast departure from our American standard. What defines so many of us—our strict calibration of activities and appointments and to-do lists, those badges that mark us as important and worthy—simply doesn't exist here. A weekday lunch can take hours; in fact, I am a little shocked, yet also delighted, when I attend my first luncheon (I am automatically invited to lunches by an executive at the Taj, and while I know that her interest lies not so much with me as with the business my husband can bring, I don't care; it's an adventure), to see that none of the guests is looking at his or her cell phone. Granted, smartphones haven't arrived en masse in this part of India, the way they have back in the States. Most everyone carries a cheap Nokia on which texting (SMSing, as they call it) can take *minutes* longer for a simple message as you click through the number pad for the appropriate letters. This agonizing slowness, this wireless antiquity, is nearly the undoing of my teenagers, who would rather suffer an aneurysm than be disconnected from technology. We might as well have dropped them in one of those tribal villages still untouched by the outside world, so tied are they to their ability to instant-message a friend with profound missives in the truncated, semigangsta speak that is especially common with blond kids from the suburbs: *Sup, dawg. Dat you at da mall? FML can't go—c u l8r, aight?*

I attend one luncheon hosted by a prominent hotel executive —a woman so well connected, in fact, that her Facebook page is filled with pictures of her canoodling with various dignitaries, including Hillary Clinton during a state visit to India. During the three-hour affair—to which no one arrives on time except for dorky expat me—not a single text or ring is acknowledged. It is a first for me, and the most engaged I have felt in a social setting in many years.

Today marks our sixth week living in Chennai, and, true to custom, our belongings from America have only just been delivered to us this morning, fresh from the world's slowest boat. I'm still in that fog that is a combination of residual jet lag, culture shock, and the special discombobulated feeling that comes from living in a place you have to call home but which holds no familiar comforts.

I was absolutely clueless about what to pack for India, and my indecision over what we needed to live on the other side of the world was made more paralyzing by the three small wooden crates we were allotted for our possessions by Bob's company, which happened to be footing the outrageous bill to ship our things to our new home. What does one pack for the third world, anyway? It's like that annoying question people ask at dinner parties: *What would you take if your house were on fire and you could grab only one thing?*

The art of packing has never been my forte. I'm not very good with the tactical parts of life and subsequently fly by the seat of my pants with most things. I have always admired those mothers at the beach or park with their color-coordinated towels and premeasured snacks in individualized, reusable containers. Those women are amazing. They are the monogrammed, insulated lunch box to my plastic baggie of crackers.

I have this friend, Trish, who is the woman you call if you are cooking something that requires an obscure ingredient. Preserved figs, chutney, saffron—whatever you need. More likely than not, she'll have two varieties of what it is you are seeking and will ask if you are serving fontina cheese as an accompaniment and oh, by the way, do you need any? Which means that when I was faced with the daunting task of packing for seven people, with a very strict limit on how much stuff we could cart along to India, she was the first person I called.

"Trish, hey, it's Jen. So, I have a two-suitcase limit per person and three small crates I can bring. What do you think I should pack?" I paused, realizing I was so out of my element that I was resorting to asking friends how to pack, and continued feebly, "I gotta make it count. We could be gone for over a year."

This is a woman who has spreadsheets for everything: dog training, homework tips, household spending, and, of course, packing. She has even figured out the various permutations of items that need to be packed depending on the destination. I'll just go ahead and say it—she makes me a little sick. But I love her anyway, and I really half expected her to whip out her laptop and pull up her list labeled "Provisions Needed for Extended Trip to Jungle and/or India." Filed after "Pancetta."

When my normally unflappable friend replied, "Can't you just take them to Hawaii like everybody else?" I knew I was entering dicey territory. Stumping Trish on packing ideas is like listening to Alex Trebek mispronounce foreign words on *Jeopardy* —it just doesn't happen. She continued, "Jen, have you thought this through? I mean, you're going to have to give your kids *malaria* medicine. I guess I would pack a lot of repellant. Just, I don't know, don't go?"

That conversation stayed with me, if only for the lesson it taught me. This was *my* family's decision, and just because I was convinced my gut was pointing us in the right direction didn't mean that even my most loyal friends were necessarily going to follow suit. If I wanted to stay true to the course that I believed was best for us, I needed to allow my friends and family their opinion but remind myself that our own lives are up to us. I know that's easier said than done, but when most people label you nuts for having more than three children, developing a thick skin becomes second nature.

Suffice it to say, we managed to pack for India—and that conversation feels like a distant memory as I stand here and look at what we've brought. I am simultaneously overwhelmed and exhilarated that I succeeded in getting us here in one piece. It's all here, finally, spread in front of me: everything my family needs to survive for up to a year in a place about as far-flung as I can imagine. It dawns on me that Bob's company spent an inordinate amount of money to ship this ragtag bunch of belongings all the way from America. I never find out exactly what it cost, but my guilt only worsens when I unpack the contents of the crates and get a good look at just what American items I deemed "essential."

Bob stands next to me, his hands on his hips. Clearing his throat, he clasps my shoulder. "Jen? Honey? Um, how many jars of peanut butter did you pack?"

I survey the mess: the crumpled sea of packing paper and shredded newspaper littering the floor of our very small living space. Boxes cover the small round table that will serve as our place for meals, homework, games, and family meetings. Bubble wrap covers the soft five-by-seven-foot rug that takes up most of the space and will later serve as our primary seating area. It is a far cry from the shameful inventory of choices we have at home in the States: family room, living room, rec room, dining room, office, covered porch. I'm aware in this moment that we have hung our hat on what amounts to merely excess. Here, there is exactly one couch for the seven of us—a rigid, camelback sofa in a very pale and very unwise shade of putty. Couches in my house are all upholstered in the closest approximation to "dirt" that I can find. If Pottery Barn made a sofa with an artistic rendition of vomit splatter and spilled juice box, it would fly off the shelves.

As I study the debris, I understand that I have stocked up on enough peanut spread to keep an elementary school in sandwiches. I look at Bob and shrug. "I don't know. Maybe thirty?"

In that precise instant, my eyes fix on an enormous, cherry-red centipede. It skitters into the house through the two-inch gap under our front door and disappears under the detritus of packing material. It's too much to process, the possible implications of such strange critters in my home, and all I can think is that I should have packed more peanut butter. Any place with bugs that enormous and bizarrely colored isn't going to be a locale where you can buy peanut butter in abundance. I eye the door again. What else can fit under that crack? My fatigue presses down on my chest a little more, and I feel deflated.

He's a good man, my husband, so he merely pats my shoulder again, hoists a plastic-wrapped bulk-size four-pack of Jif, and hands it to Rajaram, our houseboy. "Hey, Ramadan!" Bob has an epic ability to mispronounce anyone's name. I don't care if you're a Katie or a Kalikimaka, he'll botch it. "Take this to the pantry, will ya?"

Rajaram speaks a limited amount of English to complement his native tongue of Tamil, a local dialect. His English is charmingly restricted to overly formal phrases, but he is an eager learner. I watch him finger the front of the peanut butter jar as his lips move to sound out the name of this exotic-looking treasure.

I turn back to Bob. "We don't *have* a pantry." Instead, I remove a heavy metal skeleton key from my pocket. It is exactly the kind of key Cinderella's evil stepmother carried in her pocket —an irony not lost on my own daughters, who deeply and sincerely believe I possess a sadistic, room-locking streak a mile wide. "This unlocks the storage room off the kitchen. We're supposed to keep it locked until we can trust the cook."

Ah, the cook. I know that the cost of renting this house comes with a cook to prepare our meals, and that this extravagance is something for which I should feel nothing but gratitude, but initially we naively assume that we won't need Ajit —a small, barefoot man with maybe half of his original teeth in his head, a perennially tobacco-stained linen shirt, and an obvious aversion to bathing—since our new, self-prescribed status as adventurers means we can survive on peanut butter and Clif bars for months.

As if he has sensed we are talking about him, the door to the kitchen opens behind us and Ajit pops his head around the doorframe and eyeballs the jars in Rajaram's arms. He addresses Rajaram in a series of quickly spoken words, and his eyes flit between the peanut butter and me. Rajaram bobbles his head from side to side in the typical Indian fashion that essentially translates as, *I am listening to you. And I am also confusing the hell out of you if you are American and want me to nod or shake my head like you do.*

Rajaram turns and addresses Bob. "Please, sir. Is it not pleasing to you to eat the food Ajit is to prepare for you? He is most excellent cook and will make good Indian food for family."

He smiles, revealing perfectly straight teeth not unlike a row of Chiclets. It makes me wonder if they sell teeth-whitening products in India. Bob gives me a look, and I know perfectly well he is thinking, *You're the one who packed all this peanut butter. Now you can explain to this earnest kid here why we are going to be ugly Americans and refuse his service.*

A faint scratching sound comes from the pile closest to the front door. I let out a shriek. The centipede thing has now skittered out from underneath the packing material and is making its way across the floor.

"Oh my God, what is that?" *Please don't be the Indian equivalent of a housefly or a sugar ant. Better, please just be a hallucination from our potent antimalaria meds.*

"How am I supposed to know?" Instead of doing the manly thing and bludgeoning the strange jungle insect for me with a Neanderthal grunt, Bob has edged over to the kitchen door. I swear he is paler, and he's clutching the handle in a way that makes me want to hit him in the neck.

"Did you see how huge it was? It was like a snake with a hundred legs." I shudder. In truth it was maybe six inches long, but so eerily shiny and red it looked like a lacquered sports car. The kind of insect that can bite you and cause you to die a tragic death that is later buried in the pages of your hometown paper where nobody will see it except for your mother and that one cheerleader who tormented the smart kids with her ability to do the splits up against the gym wall.

"It is so dirty here. How do people live like this? What's next, a monkey in our bedroom? How are we going to get through this?" I know I sound ugly. I am exactly the opposite of the brave, adventurous woman who seizes life by the horns.

Just then, we hear a knock at the door, then watch it open before either Bob or I makes a move to answer it. I take in the woman standing in the arched doorway in a pair of skintight jeans topped with a traditional, peacock-colored *salwar*. Her black hair falls down the length of her back, and she regards me with steady, kohl-lined eyes that glint just enough to make me wonder if she is mocking me. I will find out later that she usually is.

Her heels click on the stone floor as she glides across the threshold. She stops at the pile of peanut butter and children's clothing mounded on the carpet and fixes us with a steady gaze. I see that her perfectly manicured hands hold several pieces of paper covered in flowery handwriting.

It is Shemain.

Our landlord, and later friend and mentor, Shemain, has much to say on the topic of how people live in India, along with many other subjects. From the moment we move in, she is practically omnipresent. At first, I find it unsettling; she is one more stranger in my strange home in a strange land, telling us what to do, where to go, what to eat, and how to get it all done in the best possible way, "best" being defined as the opposite of what we have planned —or, as Shemain instructs me with her characteristically blunt delivery, "You do everything wrong, Jennifer. Come, let me show you."

In fact, I could fill a book with Shemain's opinions on how Westerners live. Nearly everything we do flies in the face of how humans should conduct themselves, according to her widely varying viewpoints. Depending on the topic *du jour*, I find her soapbox grandstanding amusing, infuriating, thought-provoking, or, sometimes, spot-on. I see Shemain as an abuser—a Stockholm syndrome–esque relationship I have to endure in order for survival—but I also detect an odd charm in her, and the more we interact, the more I see her motives as genuine and caring. I just have to sidestep her sandpaper delivery on any open wounds. I end up acquiescing to her bulldozing, and subsequently learn to see and experience an India I never would if I were navigating the country and its ways alone. Eventually our family believes that without her daily presence on our front doorstep, shopping list in hand, along with her ministrations to our blatant stupidity, we would likely perish—if not from hunger, then surely from idiocy.

"You Americans never touch the earth. You travel from your car to your homes to your malls with their linoleum floors. You fly against the ayurvedic principle that we all come from our planet's soil, and it shows in your sickness and disconnect." These pearls of wisdom are typically dispensed during a meal, her proclamations followed by a self-satisfied sip of *laban* (a yogurt drink) or fresh lime juice.

When I dare to take umbrage at anything Shemain says, she merely raises a perfectly arched brow (she tends to her thick black eyebrows with the Indian practice of threading—a painful method of hair removal that I suspect makes her cranky, since she is always pulling out hair from somewhere) and tells me how it is.

"Oh, yes, I forgot—you have the best health care in the world. So that you might cure all the disease you bring upon yourselves, no? Look around you, Jennifer. See all these old men sleeping night after night on the 'filthy' ground, amidst ruin? Shouldn't they be dead? Or does the way they live their life keep them here?"

As usual, Shemain has a point. Each morning I am awakened by the caterwauling of sounds that come from the other side of my window: The ding of the bell attached to a rickety, rusted, ancient bicycle—being navigated by someone even more ancient and rusty—pulling a large wooden cart filled with our daily garbage. Or the insistent swish of a twig broom as a wizened old woman in a saffron-colored sari sweeps the length of our street. Her spine is a perfect plank as she cleans, bent parallel to the ground each morning. I wonder if her excellent posture is a result of the practice of yoga, which is as ubiquitous in India as checking e-mails is in the States.

The caws and chirping of the mynah birds arguing in the lacy Bodhi trees outside my window compete with the yodeling of the barefoot street vendors announcing their wares shortly after sunrise. The lunchtime sounds of workers gathered around one of these many vendors' food stands, eating fragrant *mirchi vada, bhelpuri, baturi,* and various char-grilled tandoori fare remind me that every meal centers on regionally grown *pulses* (a word for legumes that I love using; adopting the vernacular here, even in English, makes me feel like a local), fruits, and vegetables, and the meat is raised and killed by nearby farmers. The idea of steroids and antibiotics for animals is absurd, as evidenced by the scrawny chickens scampering away from the butcher's knife.

We are what we eat—and when I think of some of the things I used to allow my children to consume, I want to wear a hairshirt of mother's guilt over their steady diet of convenience: overly processed grains, hormone-pumped meat, and snacks containing merely a whisper of their origin—fruit snacks made with no fruit, cheese made from oil, chicken "nuggets" made from some God-only-knows confection of chicken parts and chemical foam deep-fried in a bath of trans fats. I love our new meals—always fresh, always made from something grown or raised nearby, always simple. And, most importantly, I like that we eat these meals together as a family.

"I see your *things* have arrived. Excellent." Shemain waves the shopping list in her hand as she gingerly steps over our sad pile of possessions. I wonder if she thinks this is all we have and that we are the luckiest family in the world to come and live in the Frangi House.

"Rajaram!" She claps her hands together impatiently. "Rajaram, hurry up now and clean this mess." She then says something quickly in Tamil, and he sheepishly scoops up another armload and scurries into the kitchen.

"Bhai!" Ajit steps out from behind the kitchen door, where he has clearly been hiding. Bhai (pronounced *Bi-ya*) means "brother" in Hindi, but make no mistake: Shemain doesn't consider this man a brother. She grew up with a household full of staff and has none of the liberal-American guilt that prevents me from being bossy or clipped with those hired to help me do things I usually accomplish on my own back home.

"Bhai, where is the tea? Put out a tea, now. And make a small omelet with the biscuits; I am famished."

"Oh, wow, that sounds good. Can you ask him to put some of those green chilies in it?" The cook thinks I'm a blithering idiot because I mostly mime what I want from him while throwing in the few Hindi phrases I can conjure from my guidebook. This morning, I tried to act out "oatmeal," since I needed something I could hide Henry's antimalaria medicine in. After several failed renditions, in which I was—in my mind, at least—Wilford Brimley on a horse (until I remembered they don't get American commercials or television here), a baby eating cereal, and then a badly drawn picture of oats on the back of some packing paper, Ajit finally looked at me and picked a piece of tobacco out of his teeth. "You want porridge? Just say so." It was worse than playing charades in the 'burbs after too many glasses of chardonnay and accidentally acting out that your neighbor is sleeping with your host's husband. I can't wait for the Internet to work—if only because, in the absence of Google, I am faced with the fact that I have retained almost nothing.

"Oh my God, no. Absolutely not. Jennifer, you have far too much fire in you. You need balance. You should have curd. Spicy food will only feed your fire," Shemain says.

I don't know why, but I accept this. When I'm on my home turf, I am Alpha Mom. I know what I'm doing, I know what the kids like to eat, I know how to make dinner, even if it means a quick trip to the drive-through to pick up some chicken strips and a few grilled cheese sandwiches and fries on the way to baseball practice.

But that's the thing—they don't play baseball here in India. There aren't any drive-throughs, I don't have a PTA meeting to get to, I don't have anything but this damn pile of stuff from the United States that Shemain is about to tell me is useless—and again, she will be right. Living in a world completely different from your own makes you feel like a small, helpless child. This won't last for long, and I know it, but it feels good to have a private tantrum in my head.

Shemain takes a sip of the hot, cardamom and honey–infused tea that Rajaram sets in front of us and says, "Which reminds me: you will start your yoga today. I have very special treat for you. Shall Chloe join you? She may as well know how to do things here." She sets her cup down and gives Rajaram a look. He backs out and reappears within seconds with a bamboo tray. On top of a large, flat banana leaf are two white plates, each with a steaming cheese omelet. I see no chilies.

After we eat, I change for yoga and promise Chloe that it can't be too different from the yoga classes we've taken in the past at the Brentwood YMCA. We nicknamed our instructor back home

Hot Yoga Barbie. She was twenty-something and completely devoid of body fat (except for what filled her pink sports bra), and she powered through an hour of yoga that left us sore for days. We are totally ill-prepared to try the ancient practice in its birthplace, India.

"Jennifer, Chloe, meet Gul," Shemain sys, by way of introducing us to our instructor, who is waiting for us on the small porch off my bedroom. "She lives at the Krishnamacharya Yoga Mandiram near my house. It is an honor that she is even here—she usually accepts students only at KYM—but I told her you hardly know how to get to the market on your own, so I bring her to you."

Gul is fantastic. She is so completely the antithesis of Hot Yoga Barbie that I have to stifle a giggle. I want to take her picture right then and there. Her flowy linen pants and top are the kind I wish I could wear but that would make me look pregnant or like I had on ill-fitting medical scrubs made of burlap. Gul looks as if she should be sitting on a mountaintop in full lotus position. Her dark hair is pulled back from her face, which is bare save for her heavily lined eyes—which, instead of looking overdone and wildly inappropriate, suit her exactly. (Meanwhile, whenever I've tried to emulate the India look with kohl, I've just ended up looking like Joan Jett's not-so-cool half sister).

She gives us a small smile, revealing teeth stained reddish, which, I later learn, is from chewing tins of ruby-colored betel nuts. I wonder if Rajaram could spare some of whatever he is using to have such beautiful white teeth but then stop myself, realizing I notice everyone's teeth here only because it is so entrenched in the American collective consciousness that everyone should have two perfect rows; it's tantamount to child abuse, or at least an unpatriotic act, to not spend thousands of dollars on our children's mouths.

"Please. Sit." Flowy-Linen Anti-Barbie gestures toward the ground.

Chloe and I obediently sit on our spongy yoga mats and cross our legs. Will she help me with my Downward Dog? Will I get flexible more quickly here, since it's so hot? How much weight will I lose? I am giddy with the possibility of resuming some kind of exercise routine.

Gul crosses her feet, which, I note, aren't much cleaner than the cook's, although she has the most perfectly spaced toes I've ever seen. She places her henna-whorled hands on her knees and looks at Chloe. "I ask of you, are you menstruating?"

I can feel the slow death in my daughter. She is the world's most private child about anything relating to body fluids or self-care. She shoots me a look, and I see that her eyes are wide.

"Uh, Mom?"

"She hasn't started her period yet," I answer for my daughter, who looks ready to bolt. *Let's get to the backbends already.*

"I see. And you, madam? Are you currently . . . how do you say?" She looks over at Shemain.

"Jennifer, are you bleeding?" Shemain is cool as a cucumber over all this talk of the state of our uteruses. It doesn't faze me, either, but I really want Chloe to stick around for our first authentic yoga experience.

"Nope. We are good to go." I make a little clicking sound with my mouth as I say this and point my fingers like a gun. It elicits no response. India greets my sense of humor with either flatness or confusion—never with what I *really* want to hear, which is that I should scrap everything and take my show on the road.

Gul closes her eyes. "I want you to both close your eyes and focus on your body. Please, stretch out on your mats.

"Now, I want you to breath from your chakras. Inhale. Deeply, please. Hold your air in your lungs and exhale slowly.

"Inhale now, only I want you to inhale as if from your crown chakra. This is the top of your head. And exhale."

We inhale, exhale, and hold our breath through our chakras, and I quickly realize that I am not going to be powering my way through a sun salutation anytime soon. As impatient as I am to get my workout on, I feel a growing sense of calm and peace emanating from my stomach, I can feel my shoulders relax into the mat, and I am so busy figuring out how exactly one breathes through a chakra that the normal chatter inside my head is for once not distracting me.

"Now, breathe in through your sacrum chakra. Imagine your vagina deeply inhaling. Deeper. Deeper. Now slowly exhale out; you are as if like a flower, opening."

I take a chance and open my eyes.

My daughter is nowhere to be found.

CHAPTER 5

"Oh my God. Jen. *Jen!* Peggy is smelling Dad's pants again."

I never had a household staff growing up in Oregon, unless you count the brief interlude when Crazy Peggy was around. When my mom went back to work, she broke down and hired a once-a-week housekeeper. Crazy Peggy was known equally for her amazing chili-cornbread muffins and for the creepy, semiobsessive crush she had on my dad. No offense to my dad, who was and is a good-looking man, but let's be honest: thinking of your parents as sexual beings who are crush-worthy is how we end up in therapy. It's in the same category as seeing your teacher at the grocery store or hearing a recording of your own voice for the first time—out of place and a little soul-crushing.

Around the time of Crazy Peggy's tenure with our family, my dad was a bitterly jaded state patrol officer who wore cheap brown polyester suits to work at his job as a sergeant. We caught Crazy Peggy on more than one occasion in his closet, his Sears work pants pressed against her face, letting out embarrassing moaning sounds as she backed against his shoe tree. My sister, Sarah, and I would watch her from behind the pocket door in our mom's bathroom. It was titillating and at the same time made us feel a little funny inside. Why would she make those sounds? Was she sick? Maybe she just didn't like the smell of Old Spice and Copenhagen chewing tobacco—but if that was true, why did she continue to smell his stuff?

If it hadn't been for those muffins, we might have let her go right away. But our family also possessed a high threshold for things that lived outside the box. My father had found his opposite in my mother. She was his perfect foil as an opera-singing, artistic, free-spirited woman. In hindsight, I can appreciate her open-mindedness and relaxed curiosity, but as a seventh-grade girl, I found it entirely horrifying. It was no surprise that on You and Your Changing Body Day at school, she was there as an involved mom and parent volunteer. Our class had been segregated into boys and girls, and I remember sitting in the room with my friends, painfully aware that my mother was watching over us as we were forced to view an old film reel on human sexuality.

After the lights clicked on, the health teacher asked us if we had any questions. Naturally, no one raised her hand. That day in 1983 is forever seared onto my psyche: Time slowed down in the way nightmares do—all open-mouthed silent screams and feet stuck while trying to run—as I watched my mom make her way to the front of the room. I sank as low as I could in my seat, holding out hope that she was leaving, when I saw that it was too late—she was addressing the class.

"Girls. Come on, now," she projected with the force of the ironclad diaphragm unique to opera singers. "Surely *one* of you has a question." She looked around expectantly, totally unaware that my face had melted off in shame. Should I bolt? Before I could imagine life with my new, adoptive parents, I realized with sickness that she was *still talking.* "Okay, ladies. Who here can tell me the difference between, say, menstruation"—she drew it out, like *menstrooation*—"and masturbation?"

Understandably, a pants-smelling housekeeper may have been beyond the pale for many families, but we took things like that in comparative stride—if anything, just for survival.

My husband, on the other hand, had a slightly different upbringing. Both of his parents embodied the '80s corporate wet dream—the one that involves shoulder pads, expense accounts, mineral water, and phrases like *mergers and acquisitions.* To me, there was nothing more glamorous than their trilevel 1978 home in the quiet capital town of Salem, Oregon. They had vertical blinds made of long, silky cords that opened with a remote control. Their sunken living room had carpet that went partway up the walls. And they had Diane, a whip-thin woman with tightly permed, long brown hair coiffed into a pre–Billy Ray Cyrus mullet who was never without a Virginia Slim dangling from her pursed mouth. In addition to cleaning the family's house every day, she did things like iron pants and pick up after my husband and his brother while their parents were away, paying for the shoulder pads.

None of this did anything to prepare us for having a staff in India. There is no better way to sound like an imperious snob to your American friends back home than to reference your domestics during a Skype conversation. It is nothing like the

JENNIFER HILLMAN-MAGNUSON

movies, with their white-gloved butlers and maids in black dresses. Maybe some people live this way, but for the average Western expat, having help is a normal part of Indian life, so here we are in our new rental home that comes complete with a live-in cook and houseboy, and live-out help that includes a driver, a nanny, and an ever-changing cast of characters who come and go from the house, doing everything from sweeping the leaves to keeping the water tank free of mosquitoes. The only change we've made—and it is a vast improvement on many levels—is with the cook, whom we have replaced with gentle Lakshmain.

Lakshmain is a tall, lanky man in his mid-fifties who hails from the mountains up north. He is so thin that his Adam's apple looks like a golf ball that has lodged itself just under the skin on his throat. I don't know exactly which part of northern India he's from, but I'm impressed that with his limited English vocabulary he's able to be even that specific. At this point, all I can tell him in Hindi is that I live in "thank you fish *biryani* drive slower." Lakshmain is more talented than I am, and his repertoire includes "Veddy good, madam," "Popcorn?" "Okay, okay, no problem," and "Five minutes."

Most importantly, he is able to communicate what I have to buy at the market for the day's meals; we both mime and sketch, and neither of us makes fun of the other. We've got a nice little system: he has hung a dry-erase board in the kitchen, above the ironing board, so impromptu food and household items can be drawn for the next market run. The kitchen floor is now regularly mopped and no longer serves as a bed; instead, Lakshmain sleeps in the small quarters out back, where Rajaram also lives.

It's clear that the new living arrangements are less than pleasing to Rajaram, who had the tiny building to himself while the former cook, Ajit, was here. Ajit didn't encroach on the sleeping quarters but contented himself with making a bed on a few pages of newspaper on the floor each night. Although the kitchen was never deep-cleaned during his tenure, and over time the kitchen tiles became decoupaged with layers of the *Hindu Times*, Ajit did make life a little easier for Rajaram—at least, until he provoked Rajaram into a knife fight (hence Lakshmain's arrival).

Rajaram is too afraid of Shemain to go against the new sleeping-arrangements policy and would also never think of defying our wishes, but his displeasure is obvious. I've caught him laying down sheets of newspaper behind the water cooler with what I swear is a hopeful look on his face.

Lakshmain's culinary specialties are anything in a tandoor, and he can usually be found outside (where our washing machine also resides, under a questionably stable eave that juts from above the kitchen window), stoking the coals in the little clay oven. You could marinate a shoe, throw it in the tandoor, and swear you were eating the best delicacy—albeit a chewy one—of your life. It's where the magic happens in Indian cooking.

Each morning after the laundry has been hung on a string to dry in three quick days (two if it doesn't rain), Lakshmain takes small, sticky globs of dough and presses them against the inside walls of the tandoor, where they cook. By lunchtime we have warm, smoky naan with which to scoop up our seasoned dal, chicken, or a fresh catch from the docks. The food is simple but has the power to induce gastronomical bliss—when I am eating something Lakshmain has prepared, I don't want to be anywhere else. I also know that at least a little of this butter- and curry-soaked happiness stems from the fact that I am eating food someone else is cooking for me. There is a special seasoning that is born of not having to figure out dinner when you've been doing it for other people your entire adult life. I know I will never have this kind of lifestyle in America and want to enjoy it while I can. If it sounds obnoxious to the people back home, I vow to compensate by being the kindest employer ever.

Although he is a man of few words, Lakshmain has forged a bond with my son Henry that no one saw coming. We've developed a routine where Bob and I drink our early-morning coffee alone while Lakshmain carries Henry around the neighborhood to watch for Shirmaly, our nanny. During these walks, he can be overheard talking a blue streak, none of which we understand, since it is completely in Hindi. He gestures and talks, and Henry clings to him like a little spider monkey while Lakshmain points with his long, knobby fingers to whatever it is he is waxing on about. These daily strolls help familiarize all the neighbors, houseboys, and drivers on the street with my son— something I quickly figure out when we play in the courtyard with the gate open one day. Several men wave as they walk by; others peek in and call out, "Allo, Henry!"

At sixteen months, Henry is the picture of savvy nonchalance as he continues his game with his toy car, giving a wave with his dimpled wrist but not breaking stride in his game. In that moment the bearded, turbaned, and otherwise foreign-looking men who line the street day and night, waiting for their employers to call them into service, lose their strangeness. Why haven't I noticed how polite they are? How they don't gawk like every other male in this city? How open and kind their smiles are when they see my children? I wonder how many of them have families of their own in another place. I later find out that many of them do in fact have wives and children in far-flung parts who wait for their men to send money so they can live. I'm ashamed that anything new or unknown can still elicit fear from me, but at the same time, my mental catalog of "things that are different and/or weird" is shrinking with each passing day on this continent.

As rough and unpredictable and chaotic as India can be, she is also generous, proffering up little, magical gifts in unexpected ways. Henry is still crawling, and his mainstay words include "Mama," "Dada," "no," and "cookie"—the usual vocabulary for a toddler boy who is the youngest of five and has a house filled with people speaking for him. But we soon discover that he is also picking up Hindi, likely from all the time he spends with Lakshmain.

We realize this one morning when Henry crawls over to the heavy, carved kitchen door and pushes it open with his shoulder. He babbles for a while, smiling and drooling in equal parts, as Lakshmain chatters back in Hindi from his place at the stove.

Shirmaly comes from around the kitchen table and scoops up Henry while fixing me with wide eyes. "Madam! Do you know what Henry is saying? He is saying, 'Brother! When is my food ready?'"

"Of course he is!" I laugh. "He's probably asking for his porridge, too." I go back to my coffee and e-mails. Inwardly I'm snorting—Henry is talking to Lakshmain in Hindi like I'm on speed-dial with my BFF, Madonna.

"No, madam. He is asking Lakshmain for eggs. He does not like the porridge—the medicine makes it too bitter for him."

Shirmaly is, of course, dead serious. She is the most honest, sweet, guileless person I have ever met. This also solidifies her perception of where my kids rank on the intelligence ladder. In India, so many families have only education and self-discipline to elevate them out of their current circumstances, and their pursuit of these is much more regimented than the American version. Indian kids are in school six days a week and spend so much time studying, it's like they enjoy it. Shirmaly's daughter wants to become a doctor and has recently been accepted into a specialized school that will keep her on the pre-med track. She is bright and pretty and earnest and knows exactly what she wants out of life. She is also eleven years old.

I feel like an ungrateful slug. Things like this make me regret skimming *Animal Farm* and bluffing my way through the quiz in middle school. I'm mildly resentful of my parents' vague northern European heritage—I'm sure all it's given me is a fondness for fish and a tendency toward melancholy. I can almost convince myself that had I been born Indian, I would now be splicing atoms, or at least infected gall bladders.

Shirmaly looks at our family and sees that only one of the five attends school. Maddie is under the watchful eye of the American International School, where she is a freshman. The tuition is outrageously expensive, and I am thankful that Bob's company foots the bill. It is easily triple what I paid for college. Still, I'm happy to see that Maddie now thrives in a social scene that welcomes her as an exotic foreigner. Although she generally takes a fairly relaxed approach to academics, one area where she particularly excels is in picking up foreign languages, and she has already mastered telling the Korean boys to eat her dust in their native tongue as she beats them in track practice (although Chloe shares with me that Maddie is actually instructing them to "suck it, fatty," and that even the boys on the receiving end of her invectives agree that her accent is impeccable).

It's simpler with the younger kids. Chloe is an excellent

student and possibly the most motivated member of our family. When she was smaller, my mother named her the Mafia Princess and warned us that Chloe would become either a CEO or a criminal. Because she is only in junior high, her teachers in the United States are letting her follow her curriculum online; she has all her books from school and will do as much as she can here and then take her tests when we move back.

As for Jacob and the little boys, I am happy it worked out to have them home with me. In the States, Jack would be attending preschool and Jacob would be in second grade, but it is easy to let India be their schoolroom. Each day, Jacob works on basic elementary work and then we spend the rest of the time learning to navigate the city or reading maps and planning our next excursion—and thus life becomes the classroom for my younger children in a way that no tuition would adequately cover. How to navigate the city in a rickshaw, how to bargain in the markets, how to spot bottled water that's been tampered with—these are the lessons I want my children to tuck away. Thus, I make sure Jacob comes with me on adventures around the city. Our favorite ritual is to hail a rickshaw and drive to a small café and bookshop in the neighborhood while recording the experience with my old camera.

We tried walking the kilometer or so to the café once, but even in our genteel area, it is too risky to travel on foot with rambunctious boys. Jacob nearly fell into a hole in the sidewalk that had to be ten feet deep. I pointed it out later to Shemain, who quickly schooled me on my idiocy. "Jennifer, do you not see the large stick coming out from the hole?" And I did: a scraggly tree limb jutted out from the abyss that was nearly my son's undoing. "Well, then, now you know it is clearly marked. You should have walked *around* the area."

Shirmaly says little about my four kids at home, but I know that as far as she is concerned they are all pampered truants who spend much of their day lolling about, constructing makeshift costumes, sketching, or reading books with pictures. Her inner turmoil is clear the morning Jack comes downstairs wearing nothing but his Spider-Man tighty-whities on his head—the leg holes make perfect eyes—then leaps off the bottom stair and lands on the ground, arms extended, superhero-style. "I'm Spider-Man, Mama!"

Mostly, I am impressed. I have to hand it to him—the kid is making use of what he has, and I think the underpants are an ingenious modification. I cringe only a little, but this is because of the skid mark. Shirmaly, meanwhile, gapes. Her focus goes from Jack, who is busying himself with *pew, pew* sounds, to Jacob, who is slouched at the end of the couch, his leg slung over the arm. In a moment of perfect timing, he lets out a loud fart.

"Heh. Oops, sorry, Mom." He giggles and tucks back into his *Ben Ten* comic book.

Shirmaly looks at Henry and smooths his hair. It's a proprietary gesture. Her face is creased with worry—whether for him or the other children, I can't tell. It doesn't surprise me a bit when she later tells me in passing that Henry is our smartest child. Our youngest, with his unusual ability to converse in baby Hindi, must seem our only hope.

I wonder if we are doing too much to harm the good people who work for us, as far as skewing their perceptions of Americans goes. But at the moment I'm too punchy to care much about this problem. I know it's not a good day, because I have just spent the past two hours in a funk, contemplating the loopholes in Mother Teresa's sainthood.

I mean, here I am on the same turf as the woman who is famously quoted as saying, "How can there be too many children in the world? That is like saying there are too many flowers," and I don't feel this way at all. Where is my inner peace? I want to feel like Mother Teresa; I want to look at my children and see flowers instead of ingrates. It's why I moved us here. My head hurts—I don't tolerate the antimalaria medicine very well—and the scared little girl inside me keeps whispering, *Oh, bullshit, Mother Teresa.*

I pick at the skin on my thumb and give it some more thought. Mother Teresa spent her life serving hungry orphans and sick kids. Talk about a grateful bunch. You give a starving orphan a cold compress, a gentle touch on the forehead, or some porridge, and I'll bet those kids are happy as hell. How many times did some adolescent girl hiss at Mother Teresa, "Don't touch me!" or push away her porridge and petulantly demand Taco Bell? How many teenage orphans told her they just couldn't help sweep the dirt floors because they were on their period and oh, by the way, "*I hate you.*"

I'm going to take a stab in the dark here and guess that if by some twist of fate Mother Teresa had done her service work in Orange County, California, her quotes would be completely different. Overly sentimental moms across the world would instead have hand-painted plaques above their gas ranges that read YOU CAN NEVER HAVE TOO MANY CHILDREN FETCHING YOU A GIN AND TONIC AS YOU RECOVER FROM YOUR HYSTERECTOMY. — MAMA T.

This makes me a bad person, I know. And I am trying to be

grateful on every level. I want to be one of those transformed women who return from their time in the Far East and are forever changed into ethereal, live-in-the-moment Zen mamas. The kind who stop wearing Gap button-down shirts and instead look impossibly elegant in the casually thrown-on *salwar kameez* and dangly earrings they picked up from a souk on their hiking trip through the Himalayas. Because nothing looks better with a good *salwar* than inner peace and cute earrings.

I try to focus on my view of the courtyard. It's still early, and the tiny, elderly woman who sweeps up the fallen palm fronds, coconut casings, and other detritus from the flora and fauna of our little garden is still here. I look at her closely; it's hard to tell if she's sixty or eighty. The gentle, insistent swish of her twig broom is soothing, and once again I feel ashamed of myself. I need to relax. She is wearing a sari, and it seems like incredibly lavish attire for such physical labor. Hers is the color of mulled wine, with delicate tendrils of saffron embroidery curling around the hem and sleeves. I don't know how she can move so gracefully, with such a perfectly straight spine and such clear strength.

I pull my shoulders back; I really need to keep up with my yoga. I am still seeing Gul for lessons, but we haven't gotten to the part where I get to engage in power moves or stretching. Shemain informed me that in India everyone begins the practice of yoga at age eight, and that it is years before the poses we do in gym class are attempted—that the process is slow, holistic, and spiritual. Gul is dismayed by my inability to breathe properly, and so we have been focusing on that, complete with hand-drawn diagrams that she sends home with me to practice. I contemplate sneaking in a Jillian Michaels workout on my computer, just to keep my muscles from atrophying.

I take a slow, deliberate sip of my tea—the bite of cardamom never fails to delight me—and try to ignore the sounds coming from the other side of the girls' bedroom. Lakshmain and Rajaram have nervously popped out of the kitchen with concerned looks. It's obvious they have never had the Bicker Twins as tenants, and they look to me to see what I will do.

A muffled thump emanates from the room, followed by a sound much like two feral cats trapped in a bag. Lakshmain and Rajaram both disappear instantly back into the kitchen, but I know they are still listening, because I can see their feet underneath the door.

"Stop talking about my vagina, Maddie! It's my life!"

"Well, it's not normal, that's all I'm saying."

"Shut *up*!"

"*You* shut up. It's not, or you would be able to put a tampon in. Only babies wear pads."

"I hate you! Give me back my eyeliner, *now*! You look like a total slut!"

"*Baby*. Pad-wearing baby with the weird vagina."

I take another sip of my tea. I really need to ask Lakshmain how he makes it. "Girls! Give it a rest. Maddie, leave your sister alone. Vaginas are like snowflakes: they're all unique and special. If she wants to wear a pad, you need to be quiet about it." I take a look at the kitchen door. Yep, it's as I suspected: the feet are gone.

Two things surprise me about teenagers these days. One, at the risk of sounding uptight, their language is far worse—at least in front of adults it is. I also think the reason so many of us pretended to toe the line in front of the parental units as teenagers is that back in the day, it wasn't an Internet headline if your mama smacked you for sassing her with terrible language. It might have still been wrong; it was just a little more acceptable.

Second, there really is something so much glossier about teenagers today. It's incongruous when overlaid against their language, but really, teens these days all seem to look like a magazine ad to my tired old eyes. At their age, the best thing I had going for me was my ability to memorize Duran Duran lyrics and read a *Teen Beat* from cover to cover in the time it took my benzoyl peroxide face mask to dry. My skin was without the benefits of any kind of therapy besides what I could salvage at the local drugstore or cobble from the beauty columns of my obsessively thumbed-through copies of *Seventeen*. How many futile evenings did I spend perched on the edge of my mom's burnt-orange Formica counter as a desperate concoction of ingredients dripped from my face? I *knew* I was one egg-white facial away from achieving Cindy Crawford status (as long as people were willing to overlook the headgear). I can only assume that through some alchemic twist of fate involving too much use of Clearasil, my DNA altered itself to produce the genetic mutations that resulted in conceiving children who lack the adolescent "awkward phase" gene. The only vestigial evidence of my daughters' inherited dorkdom is their willingness to prank-call restaurants and ask if "diet water" is on the menu.

Honestly, my daughters' fighting is pretty minor. I imagine that the yelling is more shocking to both Lakshmain and Rajaram because they are such steady, quiet men. I hope that if they've picked up on any English references to female lady parts, it's just the slang version, mainly because even I am cringing at how many times my girls have thrown around the word "vagina" this morning.

I take a final sip of my tea and set it aside. I will find the bright side to this little mash-up, and it is this: at least my daughters employed proper anatomical terminology. Part of being a good parent is finding something—anything—about your kids that gives you some pride in how you've raised them. Yes, some parents are able to bask in the glow of their children's trophies, and some of us are just grateful no one says "pussy."

How to Cook with Lakshmain

One of my favorite Indian staples is *biryani*, and it is too good a dish not to share. Lakshmain patiently let me film him while he was cooking it one day, and I was able to discern a pretty decent recipe based on the footage, especially considering that he speaks almost no English. If you are curious about the fragrant taste of *biryani* and aren't hung up on specific measurements, read on.

Ingredients

1 whole chicken, cut up (1–1.5 lbs cubed boneless, skinless chicken breast would also work well)

3 small onions (Lakshmain uses red), diced

4 garlic cloves, minced

1 heaping tsp. turmeric

1 tsp. (or to taste) red chili powder

3 huge bay leaves, or roughly 6 "regular" ones (the ones I see in the Spice Island jars back home are "regular")

3 medium tomatoes, thoroughly crushed (include juices and seeds)

3 large black cardamom and 4 small green cardamom pods, or about 1 heaping tsp., ground

6 postage stamp–size pieces cinnamon bark, or 2 cinnamon
  sticks

10 whole cloves

2 tsp. garam masala

1.5 tsp. salt

Dash black pepper

3 Tbsp. fresh, mashed ginger root

4 cups precooked basmati rice

INSTRUCTIONS

In a medium-size stockpot at medium heat, brown onions,
garlic, turmeric, chili powder, and bay leaves in a few dollops
of good olive oil. Bring the mixture to the point where the
onions begin to caramelize, then add tomatoes and stir. Add
remaining spices and ginger root, and continue to stir at
medium heat. Add chicken, stirring completely into mixture.
(If you're Lakshmain, let little bits of chicken collect on your
watch or the countertop, and don't worry about salmonella
poisoning. If you're not, wipe the surfaces clean as you work.)

Reduce heat slightly and let mixture cook 15–20 minutes or
so, uncovered. When chicken is done, stir in rice. If you like,
you can incorporate some diced green beans and cubed
carrots at the onion stage. I like to pick out the giant spices
(cinnamon, cloves, cardamom, bay leaves) right before
serving and garnish with diced green onions. I imagine easy
substitutes would be tofu, shrimp, scallops, or some kind of
red meat if you eat it.

Heavenly!

CHAPTER 6

The air is thick with excitement. It's already mid-November, and today is Diwali Eve. The closest comparison I have to this is Christmas—it's easily the culture's biggest holiday. It's called the festival of lights, and it stretches out over five days. Families clean their homes and celebrate the *puja*, which entails praying to Lakshmi, the goddess of wealth, and togetherness with loved ones becomes paramount during this celebratory time. The air is thick with smoke from all the firecrackers, and the banana trees hang a little heavier with ropes of multicolored lights. Every motorcyclist on the road is balancing a wrapped package, in addition to one or two extra family members.

All of this makes me excited for Christmas. Also, this morning, when Bob and I got in a quick workout, we enjoyed the fact that our tiny gym was almost empty. The gym is approximately as big as the women's locker room at my old

YMCA. In spite of its size, there is an elliptical machine, three treadmills, and an impressive array of shiny new weight machines. It's easy enough to lose weight in India if you stick to its veggie-centric diet, which we pretty much do. But if that's not enough to lose the last five pounds, all I need to do is keep accompanying Bob a few times a week to the gym, which is four stories above the ground and from which I can clearly see the construction site across the street. When I observe the male workers there, who openly and without any shame use the sidewalk below me as their personal toilet for *everything* and then go back to work as if nothing out of the ordinary has happened, it is incentive enough not to overeat at lunch. I've been to New York a lot, and even the homeless there seem to have sense enough to do their business on the steps leading down to the F train. For someone who doesn't even like her cat watching her in the bathroom, this is a little much to take.

But on this day we get through our workout without incident, and I'm excited because Bob has the day off and we have plans to eat dinner at Shirmaly's house. She says her entire street is abuzz with this news, and that the children are already planning the after-supper cricket game they will play.

When I get home, I run upstairs and peel off my clothes as I head into the shower. I don't even pause to notice the errant toilet plunger sitting outside my bathroom door. Meh. Jack is in the midst of potty training—I can only imagine what gift our son left for Rajaram that necessitates the use of a plunger. Rajaram is fastidious with his cleaning supplies. His dream is to work at the Sheraton in Mumbai, and it will require an impeccable service record with Shemain.

After a fast shower underneath a drizzle of tepid water—

thankfully free of mosquito larvae—I wrap my hair in a towel. It's really sticky and humid, and I know the minute I put on my sundress I'll be even hotter than I am now, so I start to get my makeup bag out and relish the few minutes of air on my bare skin. I look around for my hairbrush, and that's when I notice a small movement out of the corner of my eye.

It's Rajaram.

I whip around and see him holding the toilet plunger with a sick look on his face. And there we are. Me, mother of five. Pushing forty. My tummy, though now nearly flat, will never again be smooth. It is a distinct cross between peach seersucker and pulled taffy. You can't unpull taffy. And I won't go into the tired similes for my breasts. It's safe to say the whole "tube socks with marbles" thing has been beaten to death by breastfeeders who have tread before me.

Suffice it to say, were my head towel replaced with a basket of *tulsi* leaves, I would be one bottle of self-tanner short of blending in with the locals. Still, I am thankful that when Rajaram saw me, at least I was not bending over or in any way attempting to pry open a stubborn lid. After having pushed five overly large babies out of my body (all ultrasound techs ask the same question of me when scanning my fundus for the first time: "Do big heads run in your family?"), I only half joke that "going downtown" on me is, more realistically, spelunking. I can also tell you that men don't think big-vagina jokes are very funny. My husband says if I ever follow through and actually buy him a pith helmet as a gag gift, he will leave me.

The encounter lasts a second. No eye contact is made. *One, one thousand.*

In that brief moment, my emotions run the gamut. Sure, it's

vaguely violating when a stranger accidentally sees you naked. But really, I am more upset over the fact that I know I am going to have to say something about this, and that is only going to prolong the embarrassment of the whole thing. The language and cultural barrier between Rajaram and me prevents me from ameliorating our mutual discomfort with self-deprecating humor and a final "Let us never speak of this again."

And finally, I am a little sad for the loss of a body that would once have demanded a long stare, even from an innocent young man from a small village in India.

I get dressed and go downstairs. *Just relax, Jen*, I will myself. "Pretend you're European," I whisper to no one. This makes me smile. Yes, that's what I will do. I will go downstairs and tell Rajaram in the briefest and most brisk tone I can summon that he will need to knock on the doors, always, from here on out. I will be firm yet outwardly blasé. I am a woman of the world now, and these things must barely register with me. If this doesn't make me feel European, I at least feel Canadian.

Once I am downstairs, I see Rajaram by the kitchen door. "Rajaram?" I begin.

I get no further. He instantly convulses into sobs and throws himself at my feet. At my feet! The tips of his fingers graze my toes as he knocks his head against the stone floor. He manages to choke out, "Please, madam! Please forgive me!" Over and over. And over.

I am so shocked by his outburst that I am at a loss for words. I don't feel Canadian at all. So I just pat him on the shoulder and mumble, "It's okay."

Then I remember a conversation I just had with my sister about social mores in India—about how here, public affection is verboten with all but the most modern of Indians. Of course, Chennai is one of India's most conservative cities. A graze of the arm between man and woman can be construed as sexual at best, a threat or perversion at worst. And here I am, naked only minutes before, stroking this poor kid's shoulder. I want to die.

I manage to get the kids loaded into the car and take off for the afternoon. We have presents to buy, and life has to go on. It isn't until we return that I realize the full seriousness of what happened. Shirmaly pulls me aside and tells me in a hushed voice that Rajaram hasn't eaten all day and can still be heard crying from the kitchen.

Was I really so bad? Have I destroyed his vision of what a naked woman might look like? With each sob pealing from the kitchen, I imagine him shrieking, *My eyes! My eyes! How do I unsee this?*

As usual, it is Shemain who sets me straight. I immediately pick up the house phone and call her, sparing no details.

"Well, Jennifer"—she pauses—"essentially, you have ruined this boy's religion. He thought the first naked woman he would see would be his wife, someone his mother picked out for him. Instead, he has seen you."

One afternoon after the incident with Rajaram, Shemain and I are sitting at a café in the textile district of Chennai. I am waiting for her to finish her fresh lime juice and am feeling like a contented old cat, mainly because we have just come from Higginbotham's —a traditional English bookstore that is steeped in history. It is the oldest bookstore in India (and was the largest, until the 1990s) and has the feel of a Merchant Ivory film—all musty volumes and creaky wooden floors that date back to the nineteenth century. I'm happy in any bookstore, but this one feels special because it is so incongruently placed on the bustling, steamy South Indian thoroughfare called Anna Salai—as opposed to, say, in Portland. The scents of bound leather and old pages mingle with those of the livestock just outside and the street vendors' steaming carts toppling over with lunch fare, where workers eat from a few bowls that appear to be reused over and over.

Shemain takes the linen napkin from her lap and dabs at her mouth while giving me her signature fixed look through her darkly lined eyes. "Jennifer, you aren't hearing what I am telling you." She sighs and sets her napkin back down. "If you want to see India properly, you really must plan a trip with me. You are still doing everything wrong."

I take slight issue with this comment. It's not that I'm unused to Shemain's characteristic bluntness by now, but I haven't exactly been sitting on my thumbs. While the pace here is much slower than anything I've encountered before, my family's days feel full, albeit by considerably different standards. Instead of a planner crammed with scribblings and a multitude of items to be ticked off—half of which are never completed and thus contribute to my feeling that I'll never catch up—in India, I've had a "crazy" day if I've managed to get myself to the market. When I add the one-hour, sometimes two-hour, trip that is our twice-daily drive to the other side of the city, where Maddie's school sits, there is often room for very little else.

I mull through our latest adventures so I can satisfactorily counter Shemain's blanket statement. I decide to point out that we have been up and down the coast to several interesting places recently. Earlier in the month, we drove south on East Coast Road for several hours just so we could explore the former French settlement of Pondicherry. I settle on a detailed account of last weekend's trip to the beach, just for the pleasure of hopefully shattering my stubborn friend's illusion that we are incompetents.

I hurriedly swallow a fresh piece of fritter, although it pains me to not dwell longer on the crisp savoriness of this novel meal. "Ha! We were at that beach house down in Mamallapuram this weekend! How's that for adventurous?" I feel like the baby sister, making my point in an effort to be granted admittance to Shemain's sphere.

She lets her hand flop in a dismissive gesture. "Oh, you mean the hotel next to the goatherd? Ah, yes. How very brave of you." She is all but rolling her eyes at this point. "But what you really must do is come with me to the North. There I will show you majestic Rajasthan and, of course, Agra."

I'm not deflated; I know this is her way of speaking and that if she didn't like me, she wouldn't be at my doorstep nearly every day—especially since it has become clear that Shemain is a pillar in the city of Chennai, with no shortage of social opportunities. As much time as she spends with me, I know she often attends business openings and luncheons around the city. Bob and I received an invitation to her birthday gala, which was held at a local luxury hotel and packed with Chennai's finest.

I press on, no longer daunted by her ways. "Yes, that goatherd was on the beach, actually. In fact, I managed to get a fantastic picture of him with his goats. They were climbing those colorful boats on the beach." I toss her a triumphant look.

She makes a *humph* sound. "Really? You *must* show me this spectacular photo. I am surprised you got anything, given how thick with dragonflies the air is there."

It's true—the air on the coast at Mamallapuram often hums with clouds of enormous, vivid blue dragonflies. When I mentioned this to my mom, she told me dragonflies are a harbinger of high oxygen levels—much the same as moss on a tree. I now point this out to Shemain, lingering over the details, as I am really starting to enjoy antagonizing her with my "wrongness." At least she's interesting and, I note with satisfaction, at least our discourse is a refreshing departure from the typical ladies-who-lunch crowd. Instead of engaging in the bloodsport of midday gossip (if only because we have no mutual friends), we spend a good deal of our time discussing the cultural and political differences between our home countries. Mind you, America is always falling flat in Shemain's eyes, but our verbal jousting is refreshing nonetheless.

"Of course there is oxygen in the air." She makes another dismissive sound. She obviously thinks I have a long way to go before I'm allowed loose in India by myself.

But our trip to Mamallapuram is still tinged with a magical, nearly mystical feeling, and I'm not about to recategorize it in my mind as a "completely wrong" kind of place to have visited just because Shemain finds it pedestrian, so I just laugh, tear off a piece of fritter, and launch into a description of our getaway.

The hotel room we booked, just a couple hours outside the city, was inexpensive, apartment-size, and scarcely filled. It had two levels and long, spacious hallways lined with armoires for our clothes. Our bathroom was an unusually large space even by American standards—not to mention Indian standards, which are characterized by hole-in-the-floor toilets and a hose in the wall for washing. There were two side-by-side bathtubs and an old-fashioned vanity and stool. It wasn't glossy and new, yet neither was it run-down. It had the air of a place forgotten, and our relative solitude there underscored the feeling that we'd stepped into another time.

When we arrived, I placed Henry on the patio overlooking the sea and let the ocean air surround me. As he banged an old sand bucket against the stucco railing, I felt awash in gratitude. His downy hair moved with the breeze, and I could hear the sounds of laughter from the older kids, who were playing beneath our veranda. The gentle surf was soft enough that I could still detect occasional bird squawks from a nearby tree, and large, bright green lizards darted in and out of the bushes lining the footpath beneath our room.

Shemain was correct, of course: adjacent to the hotel property was a large dirt field dotted with a few dozen scrawny goats. It didn't seem strange, though—how could it, in a place where nothing looked like home?

Later, on the beach, the kids played in the water. Bob and I watched from the sand, but Shirmaly rolled up the pink cuffs of her pants underneath her tunic and joined them in the waves. At the sight of such rare playfulness from this typically reserved woman, I wanted to laugh out loud.

This was one of many moments I would have in India in which I felt as if I were inhabiting someone else's skin. I was so amazed that a girl from a small Oregon suburb got to be living *this* life. The years for me since I became a mother have been tinged with constant anxiety—somewhere along the line, my impetuous self has been replaced by a woman who sizes up baby carrots packed in school lunches by their diameter in proportion to my children's tracheas. Yet here, without the distractions of my cell phone, without several looming deadlines and the constant, nagging guilt that I was forgetting something I had volunteered to do at one of the kids' schools, I was able to briefly let go and just be. I hadn't carried my planner in months, and although I knew that wouldn't be a feasible thing to do once I was back to my regular life, this interlude had quieted the noise in my head, and in the quiet, I could hear myself again. I wasn't worried about what might befall Jacob as he dug in the sand for treasure; I wasn't hyperfocused on whether the girls' swimsuits were too revealing and thus begging for attention from deviants. I wasn't even digging for my phone in my bag to capture the moment on camera. Instead, I let my heart take the snapshot and begged the universe to never let me forget what this felt like, and hoped that the experience would help turn me into the kind of parent who wouldn't be seized by fear the next time my toddler climbed a little too high on some playground equipment.

Then Jacob was running toward me on the beach, a look of pure joy on his face, clutching a fistful of bright plastic blooms. "Mama! I found you flowers! In the *ocean!*"

His incredulity was cut short when Shirmaly quickly appeared by his side and snatched the bouquet out of his hand, her face slightly paler than usual and her normally smiling mouth set in a firm, straight line. She held the flowers with a cloth, and I noticed she was taking pains not to touch them.

"Madam! These very bad for children!" She stopped speaking English and reverted to Tamil, something I had noticed she did when she was excited or upset. After I got her to slow down, I quickly figured out why she didn't want the kids playing with the flowers in the ocean, or even in the water much beyond a good feet wetting. In addition to the water being filthy and notoriously polluted, the flowers were from a funeral pyre. In accordance with

Indian custom, countless bodies are burned and sent out into the ocean as part of a funeral ceremony—every day.

Shemain has heard enough and cuts my story short. "Yes, Jennifer, how don't you know this?" She doesn't wait for me to reply. "Because you didn't talk to me about this excursion, your children had to swim with dead bodies." She picks at something unseen on her fingernail, pausing for effect to give me another one of her stares. "I could have told you that beach is a common area for funerals."

Her earrings glint in the sun as she moves her hair. Shemain has the most beautiful jewelry collection I've ever seen up close and on an actual person. Her elaborate collection of wearable treasures makes me wonder which caste her family comes from. (Officially, India no longer even recognizes the caste system, but it is alive and well, regardless of the country's nascent policy of political correctness.) Though Shemain often goes into scrupulous detail about her life, she always seems to manage to keep me at arm's length by remaining strangely reticent about its other, more emotional aspects. Subsequently, her exact socioeconomic background remains a mystery. I do know that her family is from the North, in Rajasthan, that an auntie of hers was a maharani, and that her father was with the Russian embassy, and all that makes me think she is Brahmin.

Today, Shemain wears her long hair down, affording me glimpses of square gold chandeliers inlaid with tiny, brilliant sapphires and seed pearls. She never announces herself with perfume; rather, the tinkling sounds of gold bracelets along her arms precede her arrival. I know that most of her jewelry was gifted to her at her wedding or by family members. She shared this with me this once while letting me look through the contents of her closet, and then—as I marveled at the delicate embroidery and elaborate beading on her tunics, and as she held up piece after piece of jewelry from the boxes on the floor, all inset with the rich, robust yellow gold unique to Asia—she revealed that she defied her parents as a young woman. She was supposed to marry someone fitting after university, such as one of the polo players on her brother's team, but before the ink on her MBA was dry she ran off with a southern Indian man several rungs below her on the social ladder. It was a move that landed her in relative poverty, compared with the lifestyle she enjoyed as a child. Though Shemain's husband, Kanaan, is a highly educated man with a good job, upbringing is everything in India, and I suspect that one of her heavy, solid-gold collars represents a large portion of his annual salary.

I can't help but wonder how this makes her feel, but by now I know Shemain well enough to accept that if she wanted to discuss it with me, she would. Because she is uncharacteristically quiet on this topic, I can surmise only that it is a tender spot for her, and that if our roles were reversed, my silence would be a tactic to avoid making negative comments. All she will say is that her daily life was once so lush that her family had chefs who cooked the regular meals and specialty chefs just for the pastries and desserts. Because she was unaccustomed to having just one maid after she got married, the teachers at her young daughters' primary school scolded Shemain, openly calling her cheeky, for sending a hairbrush to school with the girls. It wasn't a mistake; she just had no idea how to brush and style their hair and was exhausted by the prospect of having to wake early to do so. In Shemain's bedroom, as I held a hair accessory in my hands that was intended to be worn along the length of a braid—roughly two feet of encrusted rubies, emeralds, sapphires, and pearls—and made a comment about how much something like that must cost, she responded, with a tinge of uncharacteristic melancholy, that money in the bank is better than gifted jewels in the closet.

I wonder if she worries that her own daughters will themselves rebel in a few short years. Is she anxious about the trail they will blaze for themselves? Will the desire to see her children financially secure in a country without safety nets overshadow her nonconformist streak and modern sensibilities? She has taken obvious pains to send them to the best private boarding school in the region, and I sense that it is a sacrifice heavy with intent.

Soon after our lunch, I am sitting once again at my table, constructing the daily market list with Shemain, when I put my pen down and grab my laptop. "Okay, let's do this," I say, clicking open the lid. "Let's go on a trip, and you can show me India your way. Just us, okay?"

A few minutes later, our airline tickets to Delhi are booked and I'm listening from the next room as Shemain calls her brother in New Delhi. I am pleased to note that even her own family is spared nothing, as she addresses him in her typical blunt fashion. She doesn't once ask if the timing of our trip works with his schedule or even if she is welcome in his home with a houseguest who neither he nor his wife has ever met. Instead, I hear her dictate our agenda: "We will be staying for several nights. I will see you then." She pauses to listen, then continues, "No—just do it, okay? Prepare your home, and we will see you soon. Good-bye."

This is how Shemain gets things done: she issues the directive, ignores whatever feedback that follows, and then tells whomever to just do it. When I caught on to her pattern and made a joke about how she should collect royalties from Nike, I was again met only with her steady stare. Once, Shemain accompanied me to purchase a crib for Henry, and when the clerk told me the store didn't offer a furniture-assembly service, I watched in awe as Shemain waved away his words as if they were annoying tsetse flies and said, "Well, then, you will come to our house and put the crib together yourself, yes?" When the stunned clerk merely looked back at her, she nodded her head from side to side and finished with, "You will just do it, okay?"

And he did. The beleaguered guy followed our car home in a rickshaw and was promptly ushered upstairs to put Henry's crib together.

The morning we leave for Delhi, I'm so nervous my stomach hurts. I'm hit with the realization that I am leaving my children in southern India so I can travel nearly two thousand miles north. Not to diminish my husband's role or the helpfulness of those who work for us, but my primary focus has always been the kids, and since most of their waking hours are during Bob's workday, it naturally has fallen to me to be the primary caregiver—a role suited to someone with my controlling tendencies. Given that I often liken parenting young children to heading a dictatorship, it works, although I have yet to experience the wake-up call that is full-fledged adolescence and so can still largely puppet-master the movements of my brood. I don't worry that my complete immersion in my family is somehow setting me up for an existential crisis once they leave home and there is no one or nothing for me to manage. I think that's because I look at myself as one of my children—I am my biggest project, although I tend to take a back burner to the other kids' needs. I see this as a plus, since my goals do not include swimsuit modeling or anything that requires a stellar exterior—I just have to keep my fingers crossed that my mind stays intact.

It's a school day, and I make sure Maddie eats her breakfast and then send Bob to accompany her in the car in my stead. As much as we trust Narynaan, it is not only improper for her to drive alone in the company of a man but also something we're very uncomfortable with, since she's only fourteen.

I pop my head into Chloe's room to say good-bye and see that she is already hard at work on her sketches. She manages to get her schoolwork out of the way within a couple of hours and prefers to spend much of her free time creating skirt and dress designs—fitting, since we are living in the textile capital of India. She looks up from her sketch pad and smiles at me; she's not yet a teenager and still greets me warmly in the morning. It's a salve, since I've learned quite abruptly that with the onset of puberty comes silence or, worse, morning greetings laced with snarls and grumbles that indicate only the teen's gastronomic needs or demand for the laundering of a favorite pair of skinny jeans.

Shirmaly has the boys downstairs, and I see her distract Henry as Lakshmain tucks the bright yellow powder that is our antimalaria medicine into his oatmeal. Jack is already in full-fledged Spider-Man mode, shooting webs at our clothes-drying rack on the patio, and Jacob has little half moons of fatigue underneath his eyes. Still, he's smiling from ear to ear as he holds out a large brown coconut to Rajaram, who delights in cutting them open when they occasionally fall from our backyard tree. He has a special knife that resembles a tiny scythe, and each time, as if on script, he cuts the coconut and then offers pieces to us, asking in his curious way, "Would Madam like some tender coconut?"

When I hear the honk of Shemain's car, I give my suitcases to her driver and collapse in the seat next to her. "Well, we're off." I set my purse on the seat between us. "The hardest part is behind us."

Shemain doesn't do mornings, so she merely nods her head. As we make our way through the crowded streets to the airport, I busy myself with the contents of my purse. I don't realize it, but I am musing aloud as I take a last-minute inventory of the contents. "Let's see: itinerary, wallet, resident papers, passport, and cash. That should do it."

Shemain turns her head from the window toward me, as if just hearing me for the first time, a look of astonishment on her face. "Passport? Why didn't you remind me to pack my passport?"

I'm numb as I absorb the implications of what she is saying. She didn't pack her passport? I sputter out, "Shemain! For God's sake, we're the same age! Why would I need to tell you to pack a passport?" But then a thought hits me and my shoulders relax. "Wait, you live here. You're a resident. You don't need your passport, do you? Can't you just use your license or resident ID or whatever?"

She fixes me with yet another stare and jabs, as if irritated by how dense I am, at her purse. "Don't you see? I am carrying a different purse. I do not have any identification."

I peer in and see that she's right. There's just a thick wad of rupees, some lipstick, and tissues. My stomach plummets. "Shemain, we don't have time to go back to your house and get your passport. I think we're going to have to postpone this trip." Missing a plane in Chennai isn't like missing a plane in the States. My confidence level sinks even lower as I remember this is an airport where cattle mingle close to the exits and even the terminal experiences electrical brownouts; the lights have gone completely dark while I've crossed a crowded waiting area trying to reach my children after using the bathroom.

Shemain looks at me. "Have you lost your mind, Jennifer? You can go on without me, and I will go home and fetch my passport and take the train. I will be there by tomorrow evening."

I shake my head. "Oh, no. I am not showing up at your brother's house without you. I have no idea how to even get there, but that's beside the point. I mean, really, I've never met these people." I am adamant. She's going to have to understand that I may be a guest here but I'm putting my foot down on this one. "We go up there together, or we don't go at all."

She nods her head. "Well, then I will just fly with you today."

It is not nearly as satisfying as I think it will be to finally look at her with an expression that says this time she is the one who is half-cocked. I blurt out, "Uh, Shemain. You can't even get into the airport without your boarding pass and ID, much less board the plane." I hold up my purse and shake it for effect. "I can't travel without my residence documentation, even though my visa is also in my passport." I shake my head, hoping the exaggerated movements are putting her in her place. I mean, seriously—even my teenagers would remember their IDs.

I expect her to look at me with chagrin, or at least acknowledge that for once I am in the right, but all I see is a tiny, maddening smile. "I will fly with you, Jennifer. You are right—you would never find my brother's house without my help."

I just turn away from her and look out the window. I'm muttering, although I'm pretty sure she doesn't care. It's not as if it matters to her that I actually have *some* familiarity with airport security protocol. I let my voice rise just a bit so she can hear me say to the window, "Uh, hello—9/11? It doesn't work that way anymore."

When we pull up to the airport, Shemain instructs her driver to take our bags out of the trunk. She is pushing this charade to the limit, I think, but I exaggeratedly shrug my shoulders and dig my phone from the bottom of my bag. I'll just call Bob and tell him to come and get us. Then I will vent to him about how monumentally ridiculous this is.

Shemain addresses her driver in Hindi, and he carts our bags up to the entrance, where an armed security officer waits. I'm practically gaping at her now. "Shemain? Really? All you have is your itinerary . . ." But then I trail off, because she is already speaking to the guard.

He regards us both and nods at me. "Papers, please." I show him my blue passport, my itinerary, and my foreign-residence papers, noting with satisfaction that he is giving them more than just a cursory glance. He is flipping to the page in my passport book with my visa, looking at the picture, then again at me. He frowns as he inspects the residence papers, running his finger over the raised seal at the bottom of the page. Finally, he nods and hands me back my documents.

Next, he looks at Shemain. She pulls out her itinerary from her purse. He waits a moment, then says, "Identification, please."

My jaw starts to unhinge as I listen to Shemain address him as she does her driver, or houseboy, or pretty much anyone else. "I do not have it. I am Shemain Thakish." He says nothing but then bobs his head from side to side and opens the door to the airport. Shemain swishes past me and goes in, leaving me with my mouth hanging open and both of our bags to haul inside.

I take a moment to remind myself that, as incredulous as I feel, she still has to get her boarding pass and make it through security. This isn't America, of course, but surely international screening measures are fairly consistent. And I *have* gone through this airport. It took us ages and involved much scrutiny of our documentation and overly long questioning for a tired family that had been traveling for more than thirty hours.

I move to catch up with Shemain, the joint burden of my midsize weekend satchel and her extra-large, old-school Samsonite preventing me from running. "Shemain, this is crazy. They aren't going to issue you a boarding pass without ID. It's *Jet Airways*, for God's sake."

She slows a bit and turns to me, watching me lurch and huff toward her with the bags, making no move to come to my aid. This infuriates me, and I yell out, despite all the people around me, "Yeah, uh-huh. Jet *Airways*. That means American rules, Shemain." She'll see. Then she can take her smug, know-it-all self and sit in silence on the way home after *my* driver comes to fetch us.

I fume while we stand in line. I'm so irritated by this colossal waste of time—completely preventable if my traveling partner would just take her entitlement down a notch and remember her wallet—I'm practically shaking by the time we reach the counter. By now I am certain that we are looking at a long trek back to our respective homes, where we will need to recalibrate our much-anticipated plans—or at least *my* much-anticipated plans. My anger is the kind born of weeks of serving my family and deferring my own needs because I know that soon I will finally, *finally*, have some time to myself.

I hand over my stack of documents with a snap and a flourish that I hope convey my extreme irritation and am issued my boarding pass. Clutching it, I move a few steps to the side. I can at least take solace in the fact that we are nearly done here. Shemain sets her purse and itinerary printout on the counter and starts speaking in Hindi or Tamil; she always seems to know exactly which of the hundreds of Indian dialects to employ just by sizing up the person she is about to address. I turn away and open my ancient flip phone to dial Bob.

Just as I hear the long, steady hum of the dial tone, Shemain walks past me, toward the security line. I keep the phone to my ear and watch her sashay confidently up to the roped-off area that is the final stop before we board the plane.

Bob picks up. "Hey, you guys get there okay?"

Before I can answer, my eyes move to Shemain's hands. She is holding her boarding pass. "I'll call you from Delhi," I say into the phone, then click it shut.

Shemain's eyes narrow in a clear sign of victory. She nods her head toward our bags. "Hurry up, Jennifer. We don't want to miss our flight."

CHAPTER 7

Shemain cements her status as icon with me when we board our flight to Delhi. As we make our way to our seats, two well-dressed Indian women in modern clothing wave excitedly in our direction. "Yoo-hoo!" they call. "Shemain, darling, it's us!"

Of course. On a plane departing a city of nine million people, headed toward twenty-five million more, two of the women in business class know my friend. Shemain glances slyly my way; I know she is loving this.

"Sanah, Daksha! How marvelous," she coos right back. She turns to me and says, "These are friends of mine from Chennai. Daksha and I once worked together at the Taj Hotels when we were younger." She addresses the women: "You must meet Jennifer. She's an American and now lives at Frangi House." I'm surprised when she takes my hand. "She is also my dearest friend."

I squeeze back and swallow an unexpected lump in my throat.

We take our seats, and I turn to Shemain. "I didn't know you used to work for Taj."

"Oh, yes. Before I met Kanaan." She smiles and leans into me, drawing her hair to one side. "You know, I was once seduced by an Arab sheikh who stayed at the hotel. He was very insistent, but I wouldn't agree to see him. Of course, this drove him *mad*, and every day he would send small gifts—flowers, or a necklace. Always chocolates." She sighs quietly. "After many days of this, I walked into my office and there waiting for me was a large, carved wooden trunk. Inside were hundreds and hundreds of perfume bottles, along with a letter."

I have no words. She must think the average American is the most boring species alive. I offer up an anemic "Wow! Seriously? What did the letter say?" I sound like the vanilla former sorority girl that I am.

She shoots me a look of annoyance. "Yes, Jennifer, of course I am serious. The letter said how beautiful I was, and how everything about me captivated him." She waves her hand in her signature dismissive gesture—as if we *all* know what it feels like to be wooed by an oil sheikh. She continues, "It said that when I first walked past him after he arrived at the hotel, he smelled me and knew that if he hunted down every perfume made by man, it would never capture my scent. He had to have me. So, to show how besotted he was, he'd bought one bottle of each perfume ever created and had a trunk constructed to fit the bottles."

This time I own my American heritage and give her shoulder a slight push. "Shut *up*!" And this time, she understands my intention. While I treasure how our differences make our friendship special, in this moment, our mutual understanding feels nice and adds a new layer to our dynamic, one in which we are just two women sharing stories.

"Oh, yes. Naturally, I went straight to my boss and we went to the sheikh's suite. I told him I was certainly not going to marry an Arab, and I ripped his letter to pieces."

"What did you do with the perfumes?" I ask, stupefied and impressed by her resolve. I would have at least said yes to coffee.

"I kept them, of course. Don't be stupid."

The moment our plane takes off, Shemain is asleep, snoring lightly against the window. I'm wide awake and excited, like a teenager skipping school. The woman on the other side of me takes out a small, round tin and offers up its contents. I politely decline with a small shake of my head and a smile. It looks like reddish-brown chewing tobacco, and even if that were something I find appealing, I have no idea where it's been. But my seatmate, like most Indians, won't take no for an answer—it's common for verbal transactions in India to involve at least one round of negotiations—and again she pushes the tin toward me. "Come, take it. It's betel nut."

All I really know about betel nuts comes from reading Rudyard Kipling as a child and from the many people here with their teeth stained the signature red hue. I take a small pinch. It's sticky. I send up a quick prayer asking not to be felled by some random bacteria in a stranger's tin. But then something inside me whispers to breathe, to take this moment of living in India and allow it to wash over me. This, after all, is what I wanted—a departure from my former life and enough new experiences to wash away the persistent, anxious feeling of a squandered existence. *Let this taste linger on your tongue. Let India linger with you,* the whisper tells me.

I hold my breath and place the bits in my mouth. My eyes widen in silent delight. It's a taste neither savory nor sweet, but more like eating a delicate incense. It's surprisingly good, belying its beleaguered appearance. I relax into my seat and welcome the perfumed taste filling my mouth for the rest of the flight.

Delhi announces its separateness from Chennai the moment I step out of the airport and breathe in the air. It's cooler by a good fifteen degrees, as well as blessedly dry. For the first time in months, I inhale deeply without filling my lungs with the moist, swampy air of the sweltering South. I am keenly aware of being near the mountains. Although it is a clear day, the sunlight is filtered through a pale white haze that renders everything slightly surreal.

I immediately start cataloging the other differences between the two cities. The streets are definitely jammed with cars and rickshaws, but so far I don't see any animals or beggars or heaps of trash. To my eyes, it feels like I have stepped into a European metropolis. I know there are slums here, but so far they appear to be compartmentalized away from other sections of Delhi.

Shemain's brother has arranged for us to have use of a driver, and she instructs him to take us to her favorite café for lunch, followed by a quick trip to the Kahn market before we make our way to her brother's villa in New Delhi. The chic café doubles as a gift shop that sells colorful quilts, jewelry, and candles. I decide to be bold and choose the avocado-and-carrot pie with rose petal–and–green apple ice cream, only because if you had asked me to invent a dish when I was a small girl, this sounds about like something I would concoct. I can't get past the first bite of pie, but the ice cream is a delight, both tart and fragrant. For her nephew, Shemain buys a bag of *agra ka petha*, a classic Indian treat made of white melon stewed in simple syrup and alum and cut into large, gelatinous-looking cubes. It looks like a lemon bar but is really a cloyingly sweet sugar bomb with an inner-honeycomb texture.

Everything appears so modern here compared with the crowded stalls of fruit, spices, and silks of the Chennai markets. I settle on a blanket stitched with hot pink, black, and orange squares of soft fabric; I'm excited by the prospect of a cool evening that might actually necessitate the use of this purchase. I'm also drawn to a pair of lapis drop earrings, but Shemain shoos me away from my selection, chiding me that I should get something different, for once. She also told me during a recent shopping trip that I was "very beige." When I confided that I still thought Annie Hall was stylish, she was visibly flummoxed and asked me why on earth I would want to dress "like a man." She now convinces me to buy some lavender glass chandeliers that look more like an Indian flower than the neutral bobs or studs I typically wear—along with my beige, black, or gray clothes.

Our driver takes us on the scenic route to the Kahn market, and as we make our way there, I drink in the architecture around me. The streets are wide and lined with buildings that lack the disrepair I'm now accustomed to in the South. We drive around the Presidential Palace, and I observe how no detail seems too small as I take a quick picture of the intricately scrolled wrought iron gates. Even the government buildings, in the North's signature terra cotta red stone, are adorned with carvings and obelisks and surrounded by old-fashioned "ambassador cars" that look like something out of a Humphrey Bogart movie. Then we approach the famed India Gate, built in 1931, a new structure in this age-old land. It's in the heart of an enormous park and bears a striking resemblance to the Arc de Triomphe in Paris. The clean lines are a swift departure from the elaborate temples and ramshackle buildings my eyes have become accustomed to over the past several months. The word INDIA is carved simply and boldly at the top, and underneath the arch stand military guards with orange headdresses and bayonets who watch over an eternal flame.

When we arrive at the Kahn market, I am amazed once again, this time by how clean and organized everything seems. I know these attributes are relative, because I have friends who have been only to Delhi, and one aspect they can't stop talking about is how crowded and dirty it all is compared with the States. To me, that impression is laughable, given where I have been living for nearly half a year. We pass fruit stalls with air-conditioning, and I snap a picture of the neat rows of colorful offerings. I'm astounded by the lack of flies, and I do a double take when I see a package of bright persimmons in cellophane packaging. When was the last time I saw cellophane? We buy sacks of fruit: hard little mangosteens in round, plum-colored shells; fuchsia dragon fruit; and ruby pomegranates with stems like tiny crowns. We pass stalls selling more silver jewelry, baskets, paper goods, scarves, lanterns, cheaply made shirts, and gaudy beaded purses (I cannot resist a purse and purchase the gaudiest one of all). Sikhs in turbans tower above the crowd, which is filled with people milling about in traditional Indian clothing and modern Western wear in equal measure.

Once we are laden down with our market finds, we make our way to the car and Shemain instructs our driver to take us to her brother's house. The trip there is more of the same visual feast: contemporary business parks, enormous statues of goddesses that are nearly as tall as some of the buildings, a large green street sign in Hindi with English printed beneath it, indicating that we are on Mother Teresa Circle.

Once we are in the suburb of Gurgaon, we stop at an intersection. On the side of the road are some discarded concrete blocks, one of which has a distinctly wedge shape. At the top of the wedge sit four small gray monkeys, and I watch them push each other down the makeshift slide, then scramble to the top to repeat the process. I know better than to act incredulous about this to Shemain, but inside I'm all bubbles.

We finally arrive at the house of Colonel Abjil Singh Rardhawa; his wife, Amarinder Kaur; and their son, Ransher (whom I will refer to as the Colonel, Wifey, and Baby Colonel, because the names are a bit hard to swallow). It is a magnificent home, all white stone and enclosed gardens. It towers three levels high and appears enormous—it would easily accommodate my large family and have room left over for another seven people. A silent houseboy dressed in cream from head to toe takes our bags in the carpeted foyer and then takes us to a sitting room with views of the back garden. When Shemain soon goes off to another part of the house, I am left alone with my hosts. It is dusk; the trees in the garden are lit with white lights, and tables are set with linens and crystal. It's a page ripped from a bridal magazine.

The Colonel has the same thick, glossy dark hair and piercing eyes as his sister. But where Shemain is about my height, the Colonel is a bit more diminutive, his eyes meeting mine exactly, even though, I note, he is wearing heeled leather shoes. He is a natty dresser, decked out in tan slacks and a black mandarin-collared military jacket with large brass buttons. A pair of gleaming riding boots is propped up against the wall behind him, and I remember Shemain telling me he used to play polo for the India Bulls. He is all smiles and grabs my hand with a series of robust pumps.

"Welcome to our home, Jennifer. My sister speaks of you to us, and we are eager to know you." Just then he turns, and I see Wifey come in through the double French doors from the garden. She is tiny and beautiful, wearing cropped ankle jeans and a casual, untucked button-down top. Her pale blue ballet flats skim against the travertine tiles, and she takes my hand in her dainty one. Next to her, I suddenly feel like a giant and wonder if my voice sounds an octave deeper as I say something about how honored I am to be a guest in their home.

"Think nothing, Jennifer," she assures me in a voice as delicate as the rest of her. We follow her lead and make our way to an anteroom filled with paintings framed in gilt, books, and an old-fashioned record player.

The first part of the evening goes smoothly. The Colonel is an avid storyteller, and he covers conversational ground ranging from Princess Diana to what, exactly, makes a Sikh a Sikh (I try to remember: a turban, uncut hair, a sword, a silver bracelet, boxers, and a small wooden comb). He finishes with the tale of the Ketchup Colonel, an Indian officer accused of faking the murders of captured Assam militants and photographing the "dead" bodies after purportedly spraying them with ketchup, all in an effort to appease his higher-ups without actually killing anyone, after they bizarrely demanded proof that he had carried out their death sentences.

After some more conversation, a brief biography of my family and me, and several glasses of good red wine (which I much appreciate, as it is near impossible to come by in Chennai), my hosts become silent. I look to the doorway and see another uniformed houseboy, accompanied by a young child who appears to be around five. Wifey makes a soft sound and clasps her hands together. "Jennifer, this is our son, Baby Colonel. Just look at him!"

I'm looking, and he's adorable. Shemain rejoins us and gives his cheeks a small pinch before sitting down. He is a tiny version of his father, wearing a carbon copy of the riding boots I saw earlier, khaki riding pants, and a crisp white shirt, buttoned to the collar. He salutes his father, who salutes back, and then clicks his heels and turns to his mother, who air-kisses him. He is now staring at me unabashedly, without blinking.

"There is a girl in my class with silver hair and light eyes like you," he says, then pauses, biting his lip. "I got into trouble because of her."

I finger my blond hair (trying not to act like I'm looking for grays—what does he mean, silver?) and nod encouragingly. Wifey interrupts my thoughts: "He tried to pluck her eyes out, you know. He thought they were toys, and she wouldn't stop howling." She gives her son a smile. "So they finally sent her home."

Baby Colonel nods his head. "Yes, and Mummy gave me a tight slap."

I'm so tickled by this entire exchange, but before I can tease out more gems from Baby Colonel, Wifey looks at the houseboy and addresses him in a sharp tone: "Girirag. Take him to bed. Now." A firm line replaces her smile, and Baby Colonel and his minder immediately exit the room, pausing only so the child can once again salute his father.

Wifey pours herself another glass of wine and looks at her husband. "Fetch my records, darling." She is slurring slightly, and no wonder—a glass or two in someone so small probably goes to work pretty quickly. Even I am feeling the alcohol's effects, but only because I haven't had any in so long.

The Colonel flinches as she slurs, but he quickly gets up and takes several albums from one of the shelves lining the wall and places them on the table in front of Wifey. She taps a long, rounded nail on one, and he pulls the record out of the sleeve and puts it on the turntable. This is apparently also his cue to leave. He kisses the top of her head, nods at Shemain and me, and says only, "Good night," before he leaves the room.

It finally dawns on me that Shemain has been awfully quiet this entire time. I give her a look, and she actually appears sheepish. She returns my expression with one that clearly means, *Eh, family. What can you do?*

This, I understand. Are we not all somewhat altered from our adult selves when we return to our childhood home? It can sometimes feel like traveling through a wormhole back in time, emerging as our younger self, even when we are grown-ups with kids of our own. Shemain is back in the North, at her older brother's house, and I decide to cut her some slack for not showing her usual alpha persona.

Meanwhile, the sounds of "(How Much Is) That Doggie in the Window," by Patti Page, fill the room. I'm pretty sure my mother had this record as a child. I stifle my smile and look at Shemain again. She breaks her silence. "Wifey? Shall we take supper outside?"

Our hostess is already up and out the door, holding a thick photo album in her arms. She stops and turns toward Shemain. "He is off to his club, you know. He can't stand to remain in his own home for too long." Shemain simply takes her arm, and we walk outside into the garden, where I'm pleasantly surprised by the chill in the air.

The rest of dinner passes in a blur of more wine while Wifey painstakingly shows me every single photograph in the album. I genuinely enjoy looking at other people's pictures, but I am struck by how curious it is that she waxes poetic all evening about her son, and shows me his entire documented development (by the time I get to the picture of the Baby Colonel taking his first steps in the Himalayas, I notice that the record has been changed to Engelbert Humperdinck), yet was so eager to shoo him off to his nursery with the houseboy. She can't stop talking about him— almost as if she were speaking of someone whom she dearly misses. I imagine him upstairs, a window open, listening to us. What would he think of my loud, raucous family? Now I'm awash in nostalgia for my own children.

Today we prepare for our journey to the ancient city of Agra to see the Taj Mahal. I don't feel any lingering effects of last night's wine—a good omen if there ever was one—and my hosts are downright charming at breakfast, never once hinting at the previous evening's strangeness. As we get into the car, Shemain simply says, "It is the same each night." She sets a book and a sweater on the seat of the car and, uncharacteristically, doesn't look at me as she speaks. "Even the records are the same."

I decide not to push it with the questions I'm dying to ask. Somehow, seeing Shemain so vulnerable tells me this is a touchy subject. She finishes, "My brother is a good man, and I love his family very much."

As Delhi recedes behind us, the haze of the city takes on the ethereal quality of a veil. Shemain explains to me that the desert is slowly encroaching on Delhi from the west, and the city is doing its best to battle the problem by planting more trees. I notice that the leaves on the trees we pass are heavily coated in a thick layer of sand and silt. After months of having jungle as my backdrop, I find the landscape as we make our way toward Agra barren and harsh. We pass huts of stone and brick, rather than dried palm fronds. Red terra cotta urns are everywhere, and even the dresses of the women are different. The influences of Pakistan, Punjab, Kashmir, Jaipur, and Rajasthan reveal themselves in the people we pass on the roads or in the backs of trucks. There are fewer saris and more *salwar kameez*. It's also true that everyone looks a little taller and broader of shoulder up here, and Shemain informs me that there is a definite prejudice that exists between the North and the South. Northerners refer to themselves as Aryans and to Southerners as Dravidians. As an Oregonian turned Southerner by mere geography, I get this schism.

We pass a lake dotted with white cranes and herons and framed by enormous, feathery brown plants. On our right is a white temple with elaborate, mushroom-topped turrets. Shemain tells me it is the Jai Gurudev temple and that a 110-year-old guru lives there.

As we approach the village of Faridabad, Shemain points to a gypsy camp on the side of the road. I see a small knot of tan tents that remind me of a Renaissance fair. Cows and buffalo are tethered to nearby trees, and as we get a bit farther down the road, I spot a group of women selling stoneware. I want to stop, but Shemain warns me that the gypsies will charge me triple and probably manage to steal my purse. Is this universal—everyone blaming the "gypsies"? I think back on my trips to France, where café owners warned me not to leave my phone or wallet on the little round outdoor tables because the gypsies would take them, just like they would pick your pocket on the bridges over the Seine without your ever knowing.

Before we are on the other side of Faridabad, Shemain tells our driver something and we pull over and park in front of a petrol stand. I half expect to see a tumbleweed make its way across the road, as we are about to enter "the middle of nowhere." Shemain says something else to the driver and then turns to me. "Jennifer, there will be no more places to use the restroom until we are just outside of Agra. I suggest you go now, as it is unsafe to stop on the roadsides."

"You bet." I practically jump out of the car. It's been only a couple of hours, but I'm in need of a good stretch and, after my morning coffee, a bathroom break. I walk around the back of the building and push open the whitewashed door. I have managed thus far to avoid using a Turkish toilet, but it is clear that, unless I wish to put on a show for the few people milling about and getting gasoline, I am about to succumb. I'll say this—it's not as easy as it seems. For a man, of course, it's no different than aiming into a urinal. But for a woman, it is a whole other proposition. The combination of squatting low to the ground, so that your rear nearly rests on your ankles, and inverting your feet just so, in order not to pee on yourself, is a workout, to be sure. My legs are rubbery with the exertion, and I am ridiculously grateful for the baby wipes I thought to stash in my purse. Not using toilet paper just isn't an option at my age.

Once I'm finished, I use every ounce of muscle energy I have to stand up; because the ground is slick with the remains of previous users, it is almost impossible to right myself without placing my hands on the dirt, but there's no way I'm willing to touch the veritable sewer over which I am crouching. My shoes slip on the detritus, but I finally manage to right myself and emerge through the door triumphantly.

I feel like pounding my chest. I have successfully squatted in a roadside toilet! I am an adventuress! Hear me roar! I inhale the fresh air with a deep breath and run to catch up to Shemain, who is standing near our car. "I've never done this before!" I gasp. She doesn't bat an eye. I continue, "The toilet thing in the ground? I haven't done that before. I feel so worldly." I'm gushing, and I don't care. This is so much cooler than sitting in the carpool line forty-five minutes before school gets out because the moms get there earlier and earlier every day so they can nab the coveted first slots. *This* is living!

Shemain is clearly willing herself to be patient with me and briefly indulges my Jane Goodall impersonation. When I pause, she gestures to the car door and says, "Yes, Jennifer. It is certainly the healthiest way to take a shit. Come now."

On the outskirts of Agra, about four hours into our drive, we pass a large shop whose windows and front stoop are crowded with various Lord Hanuman statues. I remember Lord Hanuman as the Indian god who looks like a monkey—and, astoundingly enough, the site is actually teeming with live monkeys. They are on rooftops, walls, and sidewalks, and even down the alleyways, as we slowly make our way by. Do they know something? Or is their presence just a pretty incredible coincidence?

By the time we reach Agra and are just outside the Taj Mahal, nearly six hours have passed and I am exhausted and yet also exhilarated. The air hums with energy, and it's impossible not to feel the contagious excitement. The streets are overrun with majestic white zebu bulls whose long horns are painted in blues and yellows and sometimes even tipped with bells. Wiry men of indeterminate age navigate rickshaws, and surly camels pulling painted caravans glare at passersby through their ermine lashes. After some hasty negotiations over price, we procure a tour guide and hop a bicycle rickshaw.

Our driver deposits us at an unassuming shop front. When our guide darts into the building, we follow him through near darkness up a steep stone staircase, with narrow steps that are at least eighteen inches high. Just before I start to feel uncomfortable in the dark enclosure, we emerge into what appears to be a rooftop city. Telephone wires loop like Christmas garlands above our heads, and we are led through a series of narrow cobblestone alleyways that zigzag in no particular pattern. We pass through a sienna-colored building, and then, after a wait and a security check, I am gifted my first glimpse of the Taj Mahal, shimmering through a clay-colored archway. I am awestruck.

As women in jewel-toned saris swish by me, I contemplate my pose in front of the building for my Facebook friends. (I settle on re-creating the iconic Princess Diana-alone-on-a-bench look.) My excitement at being here entirely outweighs any guilt I'm feeling about leaving the kids—and I am sure they are keeping themselves occupied without needing me, either. Henry is likely barking orders in his passable Hindi to Lakshmain about his gastronomical needs. Chloe is probably bargaining the pants off some unsuspecting tailor while jabbing at her dress sketches. Maddie has most certainly learned another curse word in Korean at her international school and will come home to enlighten my eight-year-old on the various and sundry ways to say "Screw that goddamn shit." And Jack will be passed out on the couch, steeping his Spider-Man underpants in pee as he snores against his nanny, whom he has no doubt exhausted once again. (I eventually learn to refer to our nanny as "our maid," like most other foreigners do, or sometimes even by the Indian term *amah*, as opposed to "nanny." Come to find out, "nanny" is slang for "vagina" in Sri Lanka—which is probably reason enough not to say it and well explains Shirmaly's subtle eye twitch whenever I do.)

Our tour guide leads us through the grounds while delivering historical commentary. The basic tenet of the Taj Mahal is that the Mughal emperor Shah Jahan commissioned it as a tomb for his favorite wife. He had three wives, but the first two failed to bear him any children. His third, Mumtaz Mahal, died giving birth to their fourteenth child.

Flanking the magnificent tomb are two smaller, muddy brown tombs for the lesser wives. This strikes me as funny, for some reason, and I'm feeling punchy enough to deliver. "So, they got the short end of the stick, huh?"

[*Crickets.*]

I try again: "I guess it pays to put out if you're married to a rich Indian polygamist." No one is biting at my impromptu stand-up, and Shemain turns around to silence me with a simple "Shut up." I'm not offended—I'm too busy envisioning the HBO spin-off *Big Love, Bollywood-Style* to care. Besides, I know Shemain is just more irked than usual because earlier a group of young Indian men asked to have their picture taken with me. She grudgingly agreed to photograph us but couldn't hold back on issuing her opinion: "Jennifer, they are villagers. They think you are famous only because you have blond hair."

We arrive back in Delhi exhausted and spent. My belly is still full from the roadside dinner of hot *aloo paratha*—naan stuffed with potatoes, green chilies, and cilantro, served piping hot and dripping with butter—when I finally fall into bed. I snuggle into my new quilt and dream of the Taj Mahal.

Today is our last full day in New Delhi, and I assume we are going to continue lounging and relaxing; we have already packed so much into this brief trip that my head is spinning and the memory card on my camera is full. I am constantly on the precipice of becoming used to living in India, but then something new shakes it up, and again I am miles from feeling blasé. Sometimes it's just seeing a monkey in a tree at a park, but right now it's Shemain. She is sitting on the edge of my bed, telling me our plans for the evening, and I let out a belly laugh. "*Sneak* into a function? What do you mean?"

"What I mean, Jennifer, is that we are not on the guest list for this but we are going to go anyway. Are you daft? Besides, I will know many of the people there, since my brother is, of course, invited. No one will know a thing."

"No, I'm not daft, Shemain; I just don't understand why you're so eager to go to a party on our last night. And, strangely, I failed to pack any cocktail dresses," I retort.

"I'm sure you have something black in there that you can throw on," she says as she pats my suitcase on her way out of my room. "Our car comes at seven."

I flop back onto my bed and blow air out of my mouth in a way that moves my bangs out of my eyes. I've been to a million events in my life, starting in college, all the way through work functions and country club galas. How bad can a party in India be, even if I am a stranger here and know only Shemain?

Luckily, I did pack a basic black sheath dress—and with strappy heels and an extra coat of lip gloss, I feel snazzy enough to go down to the car with confidence. But when I open the door to the car and see Shemain, who is already inside, my heart drops to my feet.

"No. No way, Shemain. I am not wearing this if you are going in"—I jab at the air in front of her—"*that*." I start to walk away. I'm a self-assured woman, but Shemain looks drop-dead gorgeous— like a character straight out of a gaudy Bollywood movie. Her jet-black hair is slicked back and secured with jeweled pins. Her eyes are lined deeply with her trademark kohl, and her makeup looks airbrushed. Her sari looks like a piece of jewelry in itself—a perfect leaf-green silk that catches the light and shimmers with threads of real gold and tiny beads made of amethyst and lapis. She is a magnificent peacock, and I am the night manager at Ann Taylor after a bender at Applebee's.

"Jennifer, darling, where are you going? You're not expected to wear a sari—you're American. Come back; don't be silly."

I stop. I notice she didn't say "stupid"; she said "silly." I turn around and look at her. "Okay, something is going on. You really want to go to this thing, don't you?" She looks surprised, as if I have just unlocked an incredibly complex riddle. I sigh loudly. "Shemain, this clearly means something to you, but you're not telling me what it is. We're friends. If it is important to you, then I expect you to be up front with me about it, okay?"

Shemain gestures to me. "Okay, okay. Please, just get in the car." She reaches down to a silver bucket at her feet. "Look, I even have champagne."

As we make our way through New Delhi, sipping our drinks in the backseat, I sneak another peek at Shemain. She truly looks magnificent. "So, what's at this party?"

She continues to stare out the window, and I see that she is running her finger around the base of her champagne flute. "Oh, I just miss my old crowd from the North, that is all. My brother will be there tonight, and all of his friends I knew growing up. Many of them play polo with him. You will have fun."

I'm soaking this in when we slow down. We are pulling into a large drive filled with fountains and lights and terraces. The building is the size of a stately hotel, although I have absolutely no idea where or what it is. I see people milling in front of a set of immense wooden doors, and I hope we are at a hotel hosting several functions at once, because these guests are all decked out.

We make our way into the grand foyer, which is several stories high and all golden lights and crystal chandeliers and ornate carpets and carved balconies. I follow Shemain up to the next landing and see a table, set up in front of a ballroom, where several women are handing out preprinted tags with names on them.

I'm suddenly not feeling so confident. "Shemain," I hiss, "this is not a *party*. This is a *ball*." I point at the plaque on the table, trying to be as subtle as possible. I grab her arm and continue to whisper angrily in her ear, even though she is acting as if I'm not saying a word and is waiting in line to get to the table. "This is an army officers' ball, for Christ's sake. The women here are in gowns, and I don't see any . . ." I trail off. I was about to say that I didn't see any white women, but I do. They are all on the arm of handsome Indian Sikhs in military uniform, and they are all wearing what appear to be vintage Victorian ball gowns, down to the tightly curled updos popular in the late nineteenth century. The Indian women, on the other hand, are decked out in saris similar to Shemain's. *No one* is wearing a sheath dress.

Shemain ignores me, and just as I am about to make a scene, she pulls me up to the table. In a move straight out of *Wedding Crashers*, she looks subtly at the names on the table below and announces, "Good evening, ladies. I am a guest of my brother, the Colonel Abjil Singh Rardhawa. And my friend here is Mrs."—she looks down briefly at the tag in front of her—"Mrs. Arjunwadkar, wife of Colonel Raj Arjunwadkar." She plucks the sticker from the table, hands it to me, and shuttles me off to the ballroom.

I fix her with the most intimidating look I can muster and say, "Shemain, you have an hour. I am going to the bar, getting a drink and some food, and hiding in the least noticeable spot I can find until your time is up. Then I am taking our car home."

I march off toward the bar. It is a visual feast of soft golden lighting and long picture windows open to show the city illuminated beyond. I really want to walk around and take notes, but my desire to stay out of a Delhi jail overrides my curiosity, so I take my drink and a plate of appetizers and walk out to one of the small balconies. I am pleased to see several large potted plants; I scoot my chair as close to one of them as possible and position myself so that I can watch the action without really being seen. I'm usually a participant in social events, but tonight I am satisfied with my role as voyeur.

I take a pull from my glass, and that is when I notice Shemain talking to a strikingly handsome man. I set my glass down and edge a bit closer, moving the frond of the plant slightly to get a better look. She is animated and laughing, and she keeps touching his arm. In my head I can hear her lectures about not touching other men, so I find this behavior very interesting. Of course I know Shemain is a flirt—I am just used to seeing her engage subtler methods of coquetry that would go largely unnoticed in America, where everything has to be brash and loud.

I have a feeling this man might be part of the reason we are here, and I make a vow to myself to not mention it to Shemain unless she brings it up, which she won't. She is married, and I still don't have enough of a history with her to go there, although I suspect that even if I did, my reticent friend would remain mum.

I turn my attention back to the dressed-up guests. I'm really surprised Shemain had the chutzpah to tell me an old black sheath would be just fine. If I could take a selfie right now, I would ironically title it *Blending In*. But I can't, so I sit back in my chair, obscured once again by the plant. I tuck in to the appetizers on my plate and dig my phone out of my handbag to text Bob.

Hey, Bob. Having fun—can't wait to get home tomorrow. Three guesses as to what I'm doing right now . . .

A BRIEF HOMAGE TO TELEVISION COMMERCIALS IN INDIA

Perhaps it's just because I'm starting to really miss American life, or maybe it's because I'm still detoxing from my former diet of a steady stream of cable TV, but I haven't ever gone this long without watching television. Occasionally, I resort to turning on the local programming. There isn't a delicate way to say this: Indian television freaks my shit out. Bollywood is essentially an incomprehensible stream of singing, bright colors, frenetic dance moves, and implausible plots centered on a love story of some kind.

The real issue, though, is the commercials. The really bad ones are these heavily lip-synced productions reminiscent of old-school kung fu movies from the '70s. Only they usually feature a skinny Indian guy with a dubbed-over voice that's incongruously deep and manly as he extols the virtues of the toothpaste he's hawking and inevitably causes a young woman to melt at his feet. Is it the gingivitis that's making her swoon?

I also get especially irked when the television doctors make wildly insane claims that would never fly on American TV. We lie all the time in America, I know this, but it seems US commercials are a little more sophisticated in the ways they brainwash the masses—allowing us to continue with the illusion that we are making our own choices, instead of promising that a new choco-vita drink will guarantee a growth spurt of many, many centimeters after the first week! (Oh, metric system, I curse my lack of knowledge of thee.)

But my favorite Indian commercials to hate, by a landslide, are those plugging countless skin-whitening products. They puzzle me, mainly because I was weaned on the media's message that the deeper your Hawaiian Tropic tan, the better—or, more accurately, the *prettier*. Of course, in the States, this concept applies only to white people, because for some reason white American people want to be tan, and people of color often, unfortunately, experience preferential treatment when they are lighter skinned. And so it is that the same paradox I naively thought was native to my country holds even in India: pale skin is clearly "better."

This idea not only disturbs me at face value but also reminds me that I have a hard time reconciling some of the dichotomies I find in India. For such a spiritual land, one universally lauded as a place of enlightenment and filled with the teachings of Gandhi and Mother Teresa, there still exists a chasm between the social classes. I am quickly learning that lighter skin here is also associated with higher beauty and most likely social status. So it is disheartening to see my late-night life-avoidance tactics (in the form of Indian news shows and old American films) interrupted by all the various unguents, ointments, creams, and serums that promise to Michael Jackson you out and make you super-*super*white.

A typical face-whitening commercial goes something like this: There is a young Indian woman. She is sad to be ugly. Why is she ugly? She has muddy, dark skin and, worse, sports a dark spot on her cheek. This renders her so hideous that she is invisible, unnoticed by even the lowly security guard at her job. Each day she swipes her ID badge and her lack of pale skin slows down every movement she has—even her hair is dull, and her clothes seem sad and shapeless. But! Thank sweet baby Krishna, she gets her mitts on some Pond's whitening cream. In a mere seven days, not only is she unburdened of the hideous dark spot—along with all moles, freckles, and other mammalian skin variances—but her face glows so white, she could be an extra in a geisha movie. Somehow, use of this cream also causes her hair to become shiny and long, and to flow in slow motion from side to side, and makes her clothes cuter and her smile bigger. Now when she passes through—nay, *swishes* through—security, our former spotted girl causes heads to turn. The guard is rendered slack-jawed, love-struck, and nearly howls with lust for her, but she no longer sees him, as an elevator of handsome, leering men waits for her.

And, cut. I miss the way Americans lie.

CHAPTER 8

TODAY'S LIST
(WITH SOME HOLDOVERS FROM THE YEARS 1998–2010)

* *Clean out junk drawer(s).*
* *Stop biting nails.*
* *Stop yelling so much.*
* *Become a better person.*
* *Lose baby weight from Baby #1 (modified to include #2, #3, #4, #5).*
* *Start yoga.*
* *Enjoy my kids more. (Thoughts? Maybe watching Oprah will help with this.)*
* *Watch more Oprah.*
* *Grocery shop.*

I think about my list. I'm good at making them: New Year's resolutions, daily tasks to be completed, the dry-erase board in my kitchen where I post our family commitments. Sometimes I get really ambitious and color-code everything. But when it comes down to how I actually want to execute some of these goals—essentially, to recalibrate my life—I realize it is always harder than just writing down my desired outcome. Every year my resolutions pile up like neglected laundry as I vow to be more of a Renaissance woman—a woman with nice nail beds, a perfect Downward Dog, and a voice that is never raspy from overuse, much less yelling at the children I took such pains to create and bring into this world.

Today I am in my usual seat on the way to Maddie's international school. We have a routine now: I load up my purse, a book to read, and my laptop to keep me busy on the lengthy journey. I'm trying to finish a blog post to share with my friends and family back home so they can see what life has been like for us so far. I bite my lip and feel a familiar sense of disappointment make its way to the edges of my thoughts. Because what, really, is so different right now, other than the fact I'm not doing my own driving? Sure, the noise and clatter of my old life are dissipating, but overall I worry that I am merely conducting our family business unchanged, only now it's happening against a backdrop of malaria, poverty, and a monumentally decreased number of life conveniences. I take a pen from my purse and scribble into my planner, pushing hard against the soft paper in my frustration.

Have grand adventure and meaningful life experiences, I add to the bottom of my list. I tear the page out of my journal. What was I thinking? That some transglobal osmosis would just magically happen for us? That our mere existence in a place so otherworldly would be the sole catalyst we needed for change, would be all I needed to reverse the ennui that had draped itself over me like a bedsheet? Well, then I need to order Narynaan to drive us all to the airport, stat. Because by that logic, all we need for lasting change and insta-transformation is to get our passports stamped in Cairo, Mumbai, and maybe Timbuktu. Then we can enjoy a few exotic meals, rack up the frequent-flier miles, and be done with it already.

This kind of thinking embarrasses me. I know that world travel has its benefits: my kids are able to get outside their comfort zone; they are meeting and interacting regularly with people who are vastly different from them. But I am still left with the nagging notion that I didn't think this all the way through.

I try to clear my head. Okay, to heck with it—I'm going to send up another prayer. Everyone needs a little clarification now and again, even from God, yes? I start to pray silently, hoping Narynaan doesn't look in his mirror and see my lips moving—an act that would likely cement me as a flamboyant and slightly off-kilter American woman in his eyes. Then I stop and remember, nearly laughing out loud. The last time I asked God for a sign, he sent me a pink car. Well, in a cosmic wink of an eye, India happens to be overflowing with pink cars. Pink is *everywhere*; in fact, I suspect it is the national color. I actually do let out a laugh as I see, right then, a pink scooter maneuvering through the knot of traffic in front of us. Either God is messing with me or the answers are all around and I am just not seeing them.

Our car hits a particularly large pothole, and my laptop goes flying, knocking me out of my pity party and to the edge of my seat. When I look out the window, I am thankful it was just the laptop—last night, heavy monsoon rains pounded our roof and lashed at our windows, and now the streets are flooded, with various effluvia floating on the water's surface. I sigh and set my belongings on the floor of the car. It's no use—if I want to type, I will need to wait until I get home, so I should just enjoy this time in the car.

I regard Narynaan's head as he skillfully navigates through the city and toward Maddie's school. I'm thankful that if he heard me laughing to myself, he didn't acknowledge it. *Okay, self, take a moment and run through the things you are grateful for*—this will snap me out of my funk. *Health, job security, all the kids are alive, and this.* If anything, even in the absence of a lightning bolt from above or a burning bush with God chitchatting to me about my destiny, I am still grateful for being here. In fact, now that I have acclimated to the *adhan*, the call to prayer that blasts over loudspeakers several times a day from nearby mosques, I am also thankful for the relative quiet of our street. As noisy as it seems with the various inhabitants, their help, and the vendors that come down our way each day, it pales next to the ruckus that is unavoidable everywhere else.

I take a quick mental inventory of what I know about Narynaan—after all, this is someone who spends most of his waking hours with us—and am chagrined to realize that it's a short list. I know that he used to test-drive cars for Ford up in Delhi. I know our company hired him and that he is a gentle, affable person to be around. He is a large man by American standards, which makes him seem even bigger here in the south of India, where men are, for the most part, quite slight of frame. His neck is thick, like a weight lifter's, and his hair reminds me of old-school movie stars', all Brylcreemed and thick.

What kind of shift must it be, from driving cars on a racetrack in Delhi to carting around an anxious American woman and her overly large brood? He's young, and I imagine we must be the most tedious thing he has ever experienced. I clear my throat. "Narynaan, tell me, have you always lived in Chennai?" This sounds lame to my ears—it's a gambit along the lines of "Come here often?" But I am still grappling with feelings of awkwardness over having people do things for me that I know I can do myself —as well as being painfully aware of the social construct here that says men and women don't casually intermingle, even conversationally, the way we do in the West.

"Yes, madam. But not in the city." He gestures with his hand out his window. "I grew up in the country, where I still live with my parents." He flicks his eyes to the rearview mirror and gives me a shy smile. "My family has several banana trees in our yard. Your boys would like to see someday? They would like to play?" The word "play" doesn't roll off his tongue easily, and I wonder if it has anything to do with the fact that I see very little playing going on among the Indian children around me.

Based on what I have observed so far, upper- and middle-class kids, like Shirmaly's daughter, are always ensconced in school. The only other youth I see are the ones from the slums. The youngest of the slum kids often walk behind their beleaguered-looking mothers, who often balance a burden on their head, such as a basket or an urn. The babies are carried, and the toddlers are either undressed or scarcely covered as they trail their families. The older ones are out trying to get food or money any way they can. It's heartbreaking to see these children, who because of severe malnutrition are even tinier than the already-small population. One day we were stalled in traffic, and I watched a child so diminutive that her head barely cleared the top of our bumper walk in front of us and over to my side of the car. Narynaan was reluctant to lower my window, as he thought he was being gallant by protecting me from panhandlers. It was one of the few times I snapped at him, and he looked surprised when I barked at him to open it.

The child reached her arms up to me. My heart lurched when I saw that where her hands should have been were badly wrapped stumps. I looked into her face—she was scarcely bigger than my three-year-old, but her eyes told me a different story. I'm sure she not only was much older than she appeared but had seen things in her short life that I would never be able to fathom. Tears streamed down my cheeks as I dug into my purse for rupees. I know how many victims of scarcity and hunger there are in the United States, but what sets my own country apart are safety nets that can sometimes help people out of tragic circumstances and a philosophy that anyone can make his or her life better. US society may suffer from classism, but that is a far cry from the ancient tradition of the caste system, which for centuries guaranteed no social mobility for the masses. The number of people in India who suffer from abject, unfixable poverty is mind-boggling.

Narynaan's eyes widened at the sight of my fistful of cash, and he said, "Madam, that is too much. They cut off their hands on purpose so that you will feel badly for them. They are liars."

The knot in my throat threatened to choke me as I handed her the money. I got where he was coming from, but in that moment of clarity, I understood better than ever where *I* come from.

My eyes are moist at this memory as I talk to Narynaan now, and I wipe at my cheek before I respond to his offer. "Are you kidding? Yes, of course. The boys would love to try to climb a real banana tree," I inch forward in my seat. I want to dig deeper and make a real connection with Narynaan. I may not know why I am here yet, but getting to know people never hurts while you're waiting for enlightenment. So I ask, "Narynaan, how do you like working with us? I know this must not be that exciting a job for you," I admit, remembering his work experience on racetracks. All I ever seem to say to him is "slow down" and "be careful."

He pauses for a beat, and I'm worried I have offended him. He shakes his head vigorously. "Madam! Working for you and Sir is the most favorite job I have ever done! You are like, like"—he searches for the word—"like movie stars."

I don't want to embarrass or shame him by guffawing at his well-intentioned but ludicrous statement. I imagine the many ways in which I can disillusion him, but he looks so sincere and kind that I decide it best just to switch topics quickly. I smile. "So, why did you come back here, to Chennai, after working in Delhi?"

He replies, "My mother told me it was time to come home." He is no longer meeting my gaze in the mirror. "It is time for me to marry."

I clap my hands together—the girl in me is always up for a good wedding discussion, and we are thankfully well off the topic of my family's pseudocelebrity status. "You're getting married? How great is that! Who is she? When are you two tying the knot . . . er, getting married?"

His makes eye contact again, with a look I can't immediately decipher. "I do not know, madam. My mother hasn't picked her yet."

Ah. So this still happens. I say a quick prayer of thanks that my parents didn't arrange my own marriage. Whom would they have picked if they'd had the ability to engineer my future? Another police officer, like my dad? A farmer? Of all the permutations of husbands my parents could put together, none comes up as acceptable, much less imaginable, compared with Bob. If the man drives me to the brink of insanity, at least I chose my crazy life.

"Does this bother you?"

"Bother me? I don't understand."

I pause, searching for the right words. "Does it make you sad that you cannot choose who your wife will be?"

He looks almost shocked. "Of course not!" He slows the car to let a bicycle rickshaw move across our path. "How would I know to pick a woman? That is what my mother is for."

I consider this. "Oh, okay. Well, do you want to live in the city after you are married?" I see this is something he is more willing to discuss.

"It is very good to live in the country. But I would like to not have so many hours to drive to my work. That would be good also." We are now at a standstill; the rickshaw made way for some cattle, and now there is a throng of schoolgirls in navy smocks over white shirts, their hair braided and tied in loops, crossing to a tan-colored bus. "But if I left my home, I would miss the children."

Have I missed something? A hidden love child? I realize that I'm craving American reality television a bit too much. "The children?" I ask.

"Yes. The children in the orphanage near my mother's home. We play football [American soccer] together. I went to school with some of the older boys. They were my friends, but I have not

JENNIFER HILLMAN-MAGNUSON

seen them as much since I finished with my own schooling and started work as a driver." He sits up straighter as he says this, and I know he is proud of his job. When Bob asked him to also serve in the capacity of bodyguard to the children because of his size, he had the same look on his face—although Shemain disapproves and tells us often that it is not acceptable to allow a simple young man from the country such access into our lives. She would probably have already died of a seizure if she knew how chatty I am being with him today.

As shy and deferential as Narynaan is with me, he is playful to the point of exuberance with the boys. With the girls, he maintains a respectful distance, but only because that is what the culture demands. After school, I usually hole up in the house and oversee homework. Invariably, during that time, he is out in our small courtyard, playing cricket with the older boys with the bright pink plastic bat we bought at the market. I see the other drivers in the neighborhood just standing around their cars during their off time, and I am glad Narynaan can stretch his legs. Despite Shemain's repeated warnings, in the long run, this relationship will prove to be one of the few areas in which she isn't right. I'm filled with a new resolve to bring our Western way of equality and meritocracy to the way we interact with our staff. I shrug off the notion that one American family isn't going to make a dent in hundreds and hundreds of years of tradition. If my hubris has gotten us this far, what's one more goal, even if it's to disassemble the caste system?

I have an idea. "Narynaan, can we go and meet these children?" I'm already picturing an outing that will keep us occupied and get us out of the city for a spell on Bob's next day off. We will pack a lunch, take some pictures—maybe even enough for a scrapbook to commemorate the day we spent at an Indian orphanage. "How many children live at this place?"

I tense a bit as I wait for him to answer. India is teeming with orphanages. Some are enormous, like mini, ill-run corporations. They are everywhere. Narynaan thinks for a moment and answers me. "Perhaps thirty? Sometimes they leave to find work, and sometimes little ones come in. It is small." Thirty is tiny by India's standards, and I relax, now imagining how our day with these kids will play out.

"Could we bring them lunch this weekend? Maybe drive over with the whole family and say hello?"

His face brightens, and he nods his head in the distinctly side-to-side Indian way to which I am becoming more and more accustomed. "Of course, madam. They will be so very happy to meet your family." He hesitates, then goes on: "My brother has a business. He could prepare the food for you to share with the orphans?" His voice is soft, and I sense that he is worried he is being too pushy by making the suggestion.

I stifle a smile; Shemain would crucify him for his boldness. "Yes, you bet. Call your brother and arrange for some food. Make sure it's good quality," I add.

I sit back in my seat. Perfect. A day has been planned. I am excited to see how everything will unfold and eager for the photo opportunities I am sure await. I document everything here, and the few accidentally good pictures I have taken have gone to my head. I paste them up all over Facebook whenever our Internet is working and misinterpret my friends' enthusiasm over the novel subject matter as my inner Walter Mitty whispers that some higher-up at *National Geographic* is going to stumble across my personal snapshots and demand that I join their staff immediately.

The call from their headquarters is surely forthcoming.

"Ms. Hillman-Magnuson? Are you the same Jennifer who posts those whimsical—dare I say fascinating—pictures on your Facebook page?"

"Why, yes. That's me."

His voice is briefly muffled, as he has put his hand over the phone to address the employees excitedly waiting outside his office door. "We've got her!"

A cheer goes up, but it barely registers with me, as I am busy petting a stray monkey—possible rabies be damned—in a park where my children cavort among the roots of overgrown banyan trees.

"We've found you!" He makes a sound that is obviously him pounding his walnut desk in triumph. "Lady, we have to know—what kind of camera are you using? We have never quite seen this combination of documentary-style photos infused with such personal meaning. Not to mention your cover shots—incredible!"

"Oh, just an old iPhone. And love, of course." I'm nothing if not modest.

"Impressive! That's exactly the kind of moxie we're looking for, Jennifer. I'm prepared to immediately offer you a contract as our adventurer/travel photographer at large. We'll pay you double what your husband is bringing in and of course will give you all the time off you need for stomach bugs and carpooling. Whaddaya say? Don't tell me Condé Nast Traveler has already snatched you up—I'll swallow my cigar right now."

"Why is this car so small, Mom?"

Before I can formulate my answer, which is a lame

explanation about the lack of enormous SUVs and minivans readily available for our immediate use because we aren't in America anymore, Jack lets out a shriek that threatens to burst all of our eardrums.

"Jack!" I whip my head around to view the kids in the small rows behind me. "What's going on? Is it too much to ask that you all act like civilized human beings for this short drive?" What am I thinking? It is easily a ninety-minute trip to the orphanage; my kids have never maintained for this long.

No one hears me—or, rather, they carry on as if they haven't heard me. Jack is now convulsed in tears, Jacob looks slightly satisfied—probably because for once he is out of the line of fire—and Henry is aggressively kicking at the back of Narynaan's seat while Narynaan patiently ignores him. The girls are both oblivious to the scene unfolding as they stare out of their respective windows with their earplugs firmly in place, no doubt listening to Snoop Dogg asking them, "Can U Control Yo Hoe?" (the actual name of one of his songs).

Jacob smiles and tattles on his brother: "Mom, Henry threw his sippy cup at Jack's head. *Hard.*" Jack's howls increase with the awareness that he now has an audience to bear witness to his indignity; as the resident fourthborn, he is already skilled in various ways to keep us engaged. The high-pitched tenor of his wailing dissipates slightly, and he pouts out his lower lip, which usually works on me. To his dismay, another sibling threatens to steal his limelight as we take a sharp turn on a narrow road to avoid a large water buffalo, causing Maddie to exclaim, "Dammit!" as her head bounces against the window.

"Maddie! Language!" I sigh. We are a mess. As usual, we are running late. Jack couldn't find his other tennis shoe, and he seems to have sprouted an inch overnight. He is happily sporting a pair of slightly too-large cowboy boots that belong to Jacob. It's crushingly hot and humid outside, but they are our only option until I can find a replacement pair. Bob and I are maintaining a tense truce, because he had made plans to catch up on some work today and I refused to reschedule. There's nothing like forced togetherness in a cramped car full of rowdy children to make for a great Saturday outing. I just want some cute pictures of the kids at an orphanage for our album, but that's obviously too much to ask of the universe, if this morning is any indication.

"We are here, madam." The car has stopped, and I didn't even notice. We are where, exactly? It looks like we are sitting in front of a tenement surrounded by several other run-down buildings.

I clear my throat. "Um, *here*, Narynaan?"

He is already out of the car, greeting a man who is standing next to a tiny two-seater pickup truck. Bob exits, too, and introduces himself to the man, who begins unloading boxes from the truck bed. A puff of wind carries a savory fragrance our way, and I realize that this is Narynaan's brother, the caterer.

I open the door and set my sandaled foot on the semihardened mud. I unbuckle the boys and help them out, admonishing each as needed: "Jack, stop dancing around, for God's sake."

He promptly bursts into round two of tears. "I'm not dancing!" he hollers. "My boot is stuck!"

I look down and see half of the too-big cowboy boot wedged deep in a soft patch of mud. I pull it out with a sucking sound. "Well, we can't really do much about this."

The girls get out next, and I hiss at them to leave their music in the car. Maddie removes her earbuds with the painstaking slowness and narrowed gaze that is ancient teenage code for wishing your parent would just die a slow and painful death already. I'm guessing she wants me to kick the bucket with a grand mal seizure, given how extravagantly she is rolling her eyes.

Bob, Narynaan, and his brother carry the containers of food and the kids, and I follow suit. We walk under a low stone doorway and up a plain, unevenly hewn stone stairway. We get to a landing, and as I see Bob push open a door with his free hand, I cringe a little more at the sight of Jack and his bootless foot clinging to his dad's leg. The door opens into a medium-size room filled with several dozen Indian children of all ages, standing and quietly staring at the lot of us. You could hear a pin drop.

Before I know what is happening, a woman in a pale green sari and a man in white cotton pants and shirt emerge in front of the children and walk toward us, their arms outstretched. Their open faces unexpectedly display the most beautiful, guileless smiles I've seen on adults, and my stomach does a small flip.

"Oh, welcome! Welcome!" the woman says in a voice that warbles as she singsongs her words in heavily accented English. She takes the sides of my upper arms in her hands and gives them a small squeeze as she does this. I can feel the happiness radiating like heat from her. I'm smiling and giving Bob a sideways look, because we still haven't heard a peep from the children gathered behind her, all of whom are still looking at our motley crew. Did Narynaan forget to tell us these children are mutes, in addition to not having parents?

The woman lets my arms go. "I am Teni, and this is Silas. We have been praying to God to help us, and here you are!"

I let my mouth drop and look at Bob. This woman prayed for a premenopausal woman in an existential life crisis of her own making, her workaholic husband, and their surly lot of children? I didn't hear her correctly, obviously, with that heavy Indian accent.

Silas joins her side and takes his wife's hand as they gesture to the children. "Our last benefactor recently told us he has run out of money, and we had no idea what we were to do. So we have been praying and praying, and here you are!"

The room suddenly erupts in noise, and as my family is swept into the crowd, I realize the children are singing.

CHAPTER 9

We are surrounded by kids. I mean *surrounded*. Also, I notice that one of the songs they are singing is clearly about Jesus—we have obviously happened upon a Christian orphanage in the Deep South of India. When one little girl, maybe eight or nine years old, finishes the song with a beautiful, high-pitched, clear voice—"Jesus, you're my superstar. Like a herooooo"—I am a little surprised; maybe I was secretly hoping for a children's song about Krishna?

After the singing is done, we are introduced to the orphans one by one. I try to remember the names, but it is impossible to keep them straight. Mithra, Revathy, Pethra, Vaiyai, Rav . . . My head is spinning, and all I can really take in is their smiles. I can feel my head being touched by dozens of curious hands, and it's mildly unnerving until I remember Shemain's nephew, the Baby Colonel, and how fascinated he was with my "silver" hair and light eyes.

The adults lead us down a small hallway to wash up and prepare the lunch for serving. The kitchen stops me cold. I have long had an evolving wish list for my own kitchen, wherever we have lived, but that seems immediately ludicrous as I take a good look at this orphanage's version—one intended to serve so many people. It is the size of a large walk-in closet, to start. The walls and floor are a worn concrete, and my first impression is that it looks like a long-abandoned bomb shelter. A hot plate is connected to a large metal propane cylinder by way of a green garden hose. A straw hand broom sits on a small pile of coconuts under the counter, which also houses a few plastic jars filled with flour and sugar. It's hard to imagine any kind of food being prepared in here.

My chest feels tight, and my eyes move to the one pop of color in the room: two small, hot-pink rags hanging to dry on a bar over the kitchen window. There is no soap, although this no longer shocks me, since I had to introduce it to Lakshmain. Even Bob's office restrooms lacked two fundamentals when we first got here: soap and toilet paper. When he initially put in his request for toilet paper, a tea boy brought him a roll on a tray and placed it on his desk. I asked him if this shocked him, and he replied, "Not really. There were schematics posted above the brand-new Western toilets with instructions on how to use them, so I figured no soap or TP kind of goes with the territory."

My own kids are silently taking in the room as well, and I wonder what impact it's having on them. I know better than to talk about it now, though, and instead I break the silence by instructing them to run their hands under the water. Bob finds a metal bowl and dumps an enormous bag of candies into it. We picked them up as an afterthought on our way to the orphanage this morning, and I see now how decadent this gift will seem. "Bob, maybe we give them the candy after lunch or something, as we leave?"

The room feels smaller by the minute, and I am thankful I don't have too much time for reflection, since my help is needed to carry the lunch into the main room so we can eat. We shoo the kids out and prepare the meal with the items we purchased from Narynaan's brother.

We return to the main room, which is by now a hive of activity and sounds, and getting hotter by the minute. I'm wearing a long-sleeved tunic over leggings, in a gesture of respect for the culture, but what I really want is a tiny tank top and shorts, it's so sweltering. Narynaan is holding Henry, who is crying; the poor boy cannot escape getting his solid little baby cheeks pinched wherever we go in India, and it bothers him every time. The apples of his cheeks are bright pink from enduring these pinches from most everyone in the room, and each time another hand makes its way to his face, he shrieks and buries his head against Narynaan's shoulder. Jack is clinging to Bob's leg so tightly I fear we won't be able to pry him off, but I catch him peering out regularly in what looks like a game of peekaboo with one of the older girls, a shy smile on his face.

When I catch sight of Jacob, my shoulders fall away from my ears. At eight, he is still very young, but right now he seems like a little man. He is laughing with a small mob of boys, as comfortable as if he were joking around with his Little League teammates. He is so much like his dad right now—all confident, easy smiles, engaging the other kids—that my heart swells with thanks for both my husband and my son.

Maddie and Chloe are already seated cross-legged on the

floor, in a thicket of girls, and I have to cover my mouth to avoid a cardinal sin when it comes to parenting teenagers; I've learned avoid all movement, including breathing unnecessarily, in order to not kill them instantly with the death knell that is maternally induced embarrassment. Maddie, who has staunchly refused to sing for us since the onset of puberty, is now crooning with several of the girls around her. There she is, singing in public with no self-consciousness, smiling as she hits the really high notes or stumbles over a word, clearly relishing the enjoyment it is bringing these kids.

The girl I remember as Pethra holds her hand up to Maddie to indicate that she should stop, and she tries to sing the last stanza of "Somewhere over the Rainbow" back to Maddie. I watch Maddie laugh and clap for her and hear her praise Pethra's singing, and I am all but thunderstruck. Just last year, when I begged—okay, cajoled, bribed, and threatened a little—Maddie to sing this very same song for her junior-high talent show, I was met with a wall of resistance and was quickly schooled on how uncool it would be to sing such an *old* song.

I am struck by how joyful I feel watching my children, and in a moment of clarity I see that by pushing pause on our old way of living and being here, my kids have more time to just be themselves. These young people aren't comparing phones and gadgets or judging each other on the external details. What is clearly coming easily to everyone else in the room is a hard-won life lesson for me, and I welcome my reawakening to the value of seeing people for who they are on the inside and discarding everything else. Here, there is no potential for the isolation that can come with parenting older children—no playgroups, park dates with other moms, or Teenager and Me classes to act as built-

PEANUT BUTTER *and* NAAN

in cohesion. Rather, the forced togetherness of India has returned my children to me in a way I couldn't anticipate.

When it is time to eat, the kids all arrange themselves around the perimeter of the room. We are unknowingly serving a fairly elaborate meal, although it doesn't appear so to us. In front of each person, Jacob places a large, shiny green banana leaf that will act as both placemat and plate. The girls and I start at opposite ends of the room, and, with Bob carrying the heavy pots of food, we ladle out individual servings of rice, dal, sambar, and mutton onto the leaves. Jack has unwrapped himself from his dad's leg and helps distribute naan. The children eat with their hands, scooping everything onto the bread, and by the time we have served the last child, they have all nearly finished.

Teni's words are still ringing in my ears. I'm not sure what Narynaan told these people, but we are not wealthy benefactors, much less the saviors of an entire orphanage. I do a quick count; including Teni and Silas and a few grown women who appear to be helping, there are thirty-seven people. I'm not sure how to break it to them that we are barely able to plan for college for the five we have, much less take on the needs of any other people.

Bob is talking with Silas, and he meets my eye, then stands in the center of the room and clears his throat. That's all it takes for the room to quiet down. "Hello, my name is Bob, and this is my family. We are so happy to be here and have the honor of providing lunch today." He claps his hands together in a gesture I've seen many times when he has addressed a large room full of people—usually employees of his. He still has our attention. "Anyone here know how to play Kick the Can?"

The children are all watching us with earnest expressions, but no one says a word. "Okay, how about soccer?" A few of the boys perk up, but then Bob recognizes his mistake and lets out a small laugh. "Wait, I mean *football*. Anyone up for football?"

The kids make a collective sound, and one of the younger boys darts out of the room, returning moments later with a battered soccer ball. Teni and Silas lead us out the back, which opens up to a spacious dirt field. I watch my children spill out, with the exception of Henry, who is sleeping on Narynaan's shoulder.

Teni and Silas guide Bob and me to a tree, where the women from upstairs are setting down four plastic chairs. I am grateful for the shade and fresh air. "Tell me, Teni: the room we ate lunch in —is that the classroom for the children?" I ask because, aside from the old linoleum flooring, the only furnishings are a wall of unfinished wooden bookcases filled with small pencil stubs, eraser nibs, and matching navy blue backpacks embroidered with the name of a copy-supply store—an obvious donation.

"Oh, yes. The children receive their schooling in that room," Teni answers. I have difficulty imagining all of the kids being able to concentrate in such a small space, with no desks or real ventilation, but before I can process how that must happen, Teni continues, "It is also where the boys sleep at night." I give her my best double take.

"Really? They sleep in there? Where are the beds?"

"Not all of them—only the boys." She lifts a small child who has left the soccer game and places the girl on her lap. "Beds? No. They have mats, and we keep them in the hall to the kitchen."

I watch the game for a moment. Everyone seems to be having fun, although I notice the high flush on my kids' faces, complete with white rings around their mouths that tell me they are quickly getting overheated. They appear to be managing so far and are keeping up, but I know they weren't raised in this jungle heat and aren't as resilient. I watch for signs of heat exhaustion as a regular part of my day now, just as I watch for symptoms of malaria, dengue, and the myriad other diseases our Nashville doctor warned us about. Even though we all had dozens of shots before we came here, they won't help against mosquitoes or food- and waterborne illnesses.

I wipe away the thin film of sweat that has collected above my own lip. Even though I'm sitting in the shade, I still feel like swooning from the intense heat. I regard Teni, who's still holding the squirming little one on her lap, and I don't see a bead of sweat on her face. For some reason, this triggers a memory of when, years ago, a coworker of mine told me he suspected that Southern socialites had their sweat glands removed to avoid looking unladylike. I know this isn't the case with my new acquaintance.

"Teni, where do the girls sleep?" I press her.

"They have their own building, not far from here. But we are about to lose our lease and will need to find another place soon." She smiles again. "Which is what we have been praying so hard about! No one likes to rent to so many children. Landlords are often unhappy to give us room, because it drives people away. So they charge us much money or make us leave." She looks at me expectantly, and I can feel her intensity. I don't know how to address this subject yet, and I can see that Bob and Silas are deep in conversation; their arms are resting on their legs, and they both look serious.

"Well, we would love to see where the girls stay, maybe." As soon as the words are out of my mouth, I realize it's more than a little bit of a hollow offer, given the heat and the fatigue encroaching upon my swiftly wilting family.

"We have a bus," she says as she moves the child off her lap.

She means that we are going to get on the bus right now and go see where the girls sleep.

"Oh, you mean *now*?" I have become soaked in sweat and have gone through the few water bottles allotted for me when I packed the car this morning. The boys have gone through theirs as well, and I calculate how much longer it will be before we are going to need more. I see a lopsided well to the side of the field, with a tattered bit of mosquito netting thrown over the top. I know all too well that even a solid tank isn't enough to keep the mosquitoes at bay and don't want to push our luck with whatever water is down that well.

Last week, Shirmaly ran downstairs with a still-wet Henry on her hip, wrapped in a thin white towel. "Madam! There are germs in the bathwater!"

When I inspected Henry's plastic tub, which we keep on the floor of the shower, I could see tiny red larvae squiggling through the water. "Oh, Shirmaly," I answered with dismay, "those aren't germs. They're baby mosquitoes."

What followed were two days of workers on our roof, bleaching the interior of our water tank and resealing the cover to keep future insects at bay. The plus side was twofold: 1) Whatever solvent they cleaned the tank with has also been keeping my roots blond—a big thing in a city where you can't get highlights—and 2) Bob and I got to spend one night in a hotel, where I took a bath in a real bathtub. I vowed then and there to never again take bathtubs for granted once I return to the lap of luxury that is America.

Teni has disappeared—I assume to fetch the bus—and I take the last liter of water from the soft cooler and gesture to my kids to come over and get a drink. All of the children see this, and the soccer game comes to a halt as the entire pack makes its way toward me and gathers underneath the lacy shade of the tree. I can't just offer my children bottled water without making sure everyone gets something to drink, but I see that someone has been dispatched to the well and several of the children are already taking long pulls from a tin ladle. I feel a twinge of guilt as I watch my kids drink purified water from the clean bottle.

"May I?" I gesture to the ladle, take it by the handle, and begin pouring water from our bottle into it. An older girl, with her hair braided in loops like the schoolchildren near our house, jerks the ladle away from me. Her eyes are wide as she shakes her head. I'm unsure what to do, so I keep pouring. She looks at the girl next to her, who has a similar look of alarm on her face.

I realize they are hesitant because of the deeply ingrained rules regarding social strata and that they are probably fearful of drinking from the cup of an older woman, one whom they see as an exalted foreigner. I study both of the girls and decide to take my cues from them, in an effort to put them at ease. I reach toward them and touch their braids. "Pretty," I say, as I let my finger slide over their mink knots. And they are lovely—these girls touched my bleached-blond hair like it was something special, not understanding how average it is. My admiration of their hair must be even more shocking than my offer of water, because they cease their protests and each takes a drink.

A loud, gunfire-like sound fills the air as a battered van pulls to the side of the field. I see that the glass from the windows is missing, although each one has two iron bars secured on the outside—I am guessing to keep people from falling out in the event of a sharp curve or sudden stop. Bob shoots me a questioning look and asks, "What's with the van?"

I pick up the cooler and sling Henry onto my hip.

"Apparently, we are taking a tour of the girls' dorms." Bob takes the bag from me as we walk. I lower my voice. "I think they think we're rich or something."

Bob leans in and responds softly, "Well, we *are* rich compared to them. And they know it, and they want us to help them."

His simple insight gives me pause, and I realize that I rarely stop and reflect on how lucky we are after so many years of struggle and hard work. Instead, I think about what is still left to do, the mountains left to climb, and this mindset has been fuel for my constant low-level anxiety. Today, I take a moment and feel happy—happy that we can help, happy that we aren't unsure about our future, and happy that we can plant seeds for more of the same with our own children.

As we watch the entire orphanage pile into the van, which is not much larger than a Volkswagen bus, I take a picture of everyone, including my kids, in what really amounts to a clown car. Teni reaches out a hand to help me climb on, saying, "It is only two streets away, and we will drive slowly."

Bob and I perch on the edge of a seat, crammed in with our kids, and he finishes his thought, whispering into my ear, "I guess what we need to decide is, do we want to help them, and to what extent?"

We pull up in front of another gray cement building, not much different from the one we came from, except the two buildings on either side of it are painted yellow and pink, the street has several trees, and the pond behind the building is filled with ebony water buffalo. Their coats gleam in the sun, and two of them raise their heads toward me. They snort out of their flattened nostrils as they move slowly through the water.

I turn to Narynaan with a rapt expression on my face, but he's quick to burst my bubble: "I'm sorry, madam, but they are very dangerous. They kill many people. Please, move back." We walk over to the girls' dormitory, where I see a much safer photo subject. An elderly woman in a vivid blue sari is sitting in front of the yellow building, her gray hair falling loosely around her face, which is unusual—typically, Indian women keep their hair tied back or up in some fashion. As if sensing my thoughts, she hastily arranges it in a soft braid down her back as we all get off the bus.

I take out my camera. "Pardon me . . . " I trail off a bit, because it is clear she doesn't speak English, so I use my well-honed miming skills to ask if I can take her picture. I am thrilled when she seems obviously happy with this idea, and she tucks her braid behind her head and smooths the front of her sari. She tilts her head and gives me a small smile, revealing beautifully sculpted cheekbones. She is sitting in front of the yellow wall, which makes for a lovely contrast with her cerulean dress, and when I show her the picture on my camera screen, she puts her fingers over her mouth in a gesture that says she is pleased; she looks strikingly pretty.

We take a quick tour of the girls' sleeping quarters, and they aren't much to see. There are three rooms, almost all bare, except for bags of clothing and some bedding. I don't see a single toy, even though the youngest of the girls appears to be around four; the oldest is maybe seventeen or eighteen, and the majority are between eight and twelve. There are no window coverings on the windows besides wooden shutters that have large gaps in them.

I ask Teni, who is leading the tour, "How do you keep the mosquitoes out?" I remember the netting covering the well at the school.

She bobs her head. "Yes, sometimes we have netting, but it gets torn very easily and sometimes it is stolen."

My family is still choking down bright orange pills daily to protect us from malaria, and I know it costs Bob's company thousands of dollars to hire a compounding pharmacist to make up nearly a year's worth of meds for seven people. I know that only the expats here take antimalaria medicine, although many eventually stop because of the side effects.

Teni continues, "What we really need is plastic netting, so we can nail it in place." She gestures to the smallest of the three rooms. "And here is where the teachers sleep. We have until the end of the month to find another place, hopefully as nice as this one."

The pride underlying her words shocks me. The place is not squalid—there is no filth or debris anywhere—but it is so primal and basic, I wonder how it can possibly meet the needs of so many girls. I suddenly realize that asking about the lack of toys would seem frivolous. My own daughters have drawn battle lines each day since they started sharing a bathroom; I wonder if they are noticing this bathroom—which contains only a showerhead, a Turkish toilet, a hose, and a small sink—and realizing it is the only option for at least fifteen girls. Then Maddie pulls on my arm and says, "Mom, there isn't even a *mirror* in their bathroom." I nod my head and take her hand as we walk back outside.

Back at the orphanage, we instruct Narynaan to load up the car and turn on the air-conditioning. By the time we get back to our home, it will be dark. I know Lakshmain is there right now, preparing fish and noodles for us—our favorite. Shirmaly will help me bathe the boys and prepare them for bed, and I will be able to tuck myself into clean sheets and read a book for the rest of the evening. Suddenly, I feel like a princess.

We shake Silas's and Teni's hands good-bye, and as we do, the children surround us again, only this time they are hugging us and giving Jack's and Henry's cheeks one last pinch. "Good-bye, Auntie! Good-bye, Uncle!"

I look at Bob and smile as he buckles Henry into his car seat. There are three or four boys sitting in our minivan, running their hands over the upholstery, and another group pushes its way into the car when Narynaan starts up the DVD player with an old episode of *SpongeBob* for our worn-out kids. Bob and I bid Teni and Silas one last good-bye and close the doors. It's like a send-off for a cruise, only we are just going home.

We call for our daughters, and for a moment I feel a pang of alarm. Then I hear a high-pitched sound coming from a circle of girls, and as I walk toward them, I see Chloe's and Maddie's yellow hair haloed in the light of the setting sun. They are all holding hands and spinning around until they stumble or fall to the ground, and laughing hard.

I hear the same squeal again and watch the youngest girl run through the middle of the circle into Chloe's arms. Chloe catches her with a growl. I don't know when I last saw my daughters behave so freely, without the mask of teenage inhibition that constantly hisses at them to stop whatever it is they are doing because it doesn't look cool. "Maddie! Chloe! Let's go!" I call to them.

They break away from the circle and stagger to the car, still smiling. "Mom, we were playing Goat and Tiger—it's like Red Rover." Chloe is panting as she climbs into the backseat.

I push her bangs out of her eyes; she looks exhausted, and a thin coating of dirt sticks to the sweat on her face, as if it were a floured cake pan, but she is grinning ear to ear and she doesn't push my hand away. "Did you have fun, honey?"

She and Maddie both give me a grin and a "yes" and then pop

their earbuds back in place while waving to the orphans gathered around our car.

Teni leans into my window and looks first at me, then at Bob. "Same time next Saturday?" She nods her head from side to side. I look at Bob, and he places his hand on my leg; I give him a small nod, and he squeezes my knee, before answering, "Yes, Teni. We will see you next Saturday."

How to Feel Like a Badass in India When You're Really a Scaredy-Cat White American Girl: A Tutorial

Are you, too, an American-born woman whose idea of fun and excitement involves getting an extra shot at Starbucks? Do you rock your bad-girl style by getting all-black clothes at the White House Black Market clothing boutique? Maybe sometimes you chill with your homegirls and say, "Screw it. No chardonnay for me tonight—I'm having a Jack and Coke after I watch some Lifetime television." Then read on, soul sister, and learn how to bring it, India-style.

STEP ONE: Go all by yourself to the textile markets with your thirteen-year-old daughter. Bravely shoo the rest of the family off to a school picnic and tell them to pick you up after. That's right. After. That's at least two and a half hours to get outside the Nungambakkam District and slum it on Anna Salai.

STEP TWO: While picking out fabrics for the skirts you and your daughter designed together (yeah, that's right, your secondborn shared an activity with you without being forced. Can I get an "oh, yeah"?), keep cool when a smartly dressed woman approaches you and asks to see your daughter's drawings. When she admires them and asks if your daughter would design a skirt for her, don't bat an eyelash as you reply, cool as a cucumber, "Give us your number. Maybe we can come up with some sketches for you." When she asks for the name of your company, do not giggle once as you say it's India Girls Couture. (The first rule of being a badass is, you giggle alone.) Act extracool when you have to administer a quick kick to your daughter's shin. This is just more badass code for "Don't blow our cover!" Don't reveal your surprise when your daughter catches on in a rare moment of solidarity with you, and don't squeal with delight when she totally goes with it and starts suggesting design ideas on the fly, using terms like "chic" and "whimsical Indo-Western fusion." Badasses don't get sentimental over bonding with their daughters, even if it has been forever since you played together.

STEP THREE: Leave the textile markets and wander aimlessly. Get lost because you are without your driver or local friend, and be okay with this. Maintaining your cool, pop into a random shop guarded by several chickens. Pick out a shawl for your American BFF and barter for it. Yeah, so what if they jacked up the prices the minute they saw you come in? You are onto them. Save yourself ten rupees on your purchase. Act like you don't care when your daughter points out that this is less than twenty-five cents. Showing emotion is reserved for Starbucks, like when they give you whole-fat milk instead of skim.

STEP FOUR: Walk around some more. Don't complain too much that it's hot and humid and that your head and feet already hurt and maybe kitten heels weren't the best idea. Don't think about what that smell might have been. Keep going. Because your driver is at the picnic. In your boldest move to date, suggest you get something to drink from a street vendor. Throw caution to the wind as you purchase and consume two orange sodas. Sure, they're bottled and look securely capped. But this is India. You just never know. Drink them; look at your sweet, precious baby, who is growing up way too fast, and think, *Her orange mustache is like a badge of courage. And I have one, too.* Nod to the street vendor.

STEP FIVE: Emboldened by your courageous beverage move, suggest to your now-pallid-and-sweaty daughter that you not wait for your family to come and get you. Rather, submit that you take an auto rickshaw home. Channel your inner Carrie Bradshaw and flag down the next one you see, NYC-style. That's right, you've been to NYC once before. Twice, if you count that layover. Try not to smirk as you instruct him in Hindi to take you to Nawab Habibullah Avenue in Nungambakkam. Don't let on that this is one of three phrases you know, and that you practice saying them in front of the mirror. You sound like a local. He probably thinks you're British. Call your husband and tell him no need to pick you up—you and your daughter are taking a rickshaw home. When he says there is no way in hell you are taking one of those rickety death traps all the way back to the house in that traffic, laugh— cackle like the badass you are—and tell him you are already on your way. Yell into the phone that you are making bold moves with your life before you hang up. Grab the side of the rickshaw for dear life and tap your foot in time to your inner Tupac soundtrack as you yell over the din of traffic at the driver, "There's an extra hundred rupees in it for you if you keep it slow."

Because that's how we roll.

CHAPTER 10

D riving up to the American International School in Chennai is like approaching a military base in the middle of a war zone. The area is surrounded by mini-slums, half-constructed tech parks, and alleyways teeming with chickens and clotheslines and cattle and naked children. The enormous physical grounds are surrounded in the front by a moat —whether by design or as a by-product of India's many cyclones, I'll never know. A large stone-and-iron fence with razor wire curlicuing its way along the very top encloses the school's entire perimeter.

Standing on a makeshift plywood bridge over the moat are at least three security guards dressed in desert khakis and carrying firearms. Every day, they instruct us to slow our car to a crawl and then to stop so they can inspect our vehicle for the appropriate stickers, passes, and passengers before they let us proceed through the electric iron gates. Beyond the gates are several more guards directing traffic—which is only slightly less crazy than it is in the rest of the city. There are no parent volunteers helping children cross the parking lot safely. There is no politesse, no gestures of "After you . . . " "No, after you—I insist." Instead, the guards blow on whistles with the fervor of World Cup referees, taking them out only to bark at the cars with the same phrase over and over. It sounds like they are yelling, *"Bullah! Bullah! Bullah!"* which is obviously some form of "Hurry the hell up!"

But most surprising of all is how, once we are through the second security checkpoint and the last set of heavy steel doors, it's like going through a portal from a scene straight out of *Slumdog Millionaire* to a tranquil, beautiful campus that is lush with vegetation. Inside the school grounds are open-air hallways adorned with papier-mâché art and paintings from the lower grades, courtyards fragrant with the perfume of climbing jasmine, and expansive green fields for soccer and other games. In fact, it is the only place in Chennai where we ever see such a large grassy space. It quickly becomes the highlight of our weekdays, our sanctuary away from the noise and dirt and hustle of the city.

It is also one of our greatest sources of entertainment. I imagine it is hard to recruit teachers for some of these international posts in obscure parts of the world where the curriculum must still be followed to maintain American accreditation—and, subsequently, some of the teachers here are real characters. My favorite by far is Maddie's PE teacher. He is a stout, barrel-chested Israeli who chomps on a perpetually unlit cigar and hurls insults at his students. He unabashedly favors the more physically fit students and takes sincere pleasure in berating and shaming the poor kids who can't keep up. He is perfectly typecast as the sadistic instructor who embarrasses the chubby kid for not being able to climb the rope ladder hanging from the gym ceiling. And, oddly, AISC is teeming with chubby kids.

At least half of the school population is composed of Korean nationals, because of the large Hyundai operations plant in Chennai. A typical Korean student here is a little soft around the middle, eschews exercise on the grounds that any free time should be spent studying, and consistently tests in the highest percentile. To complicate matters, most of these kids speak little to no English and are dually enrolled in the ESL program. Each Korean student has an impeccably dressed mother who spends all day at the school, where she passes the time sitting in the courtyard and socializing with the other Korean mothers. These women are petite and turned out in Carolina Herrera linen skirts, Fendi pumps, and Hermès bags, and they do not want to talk to the other moms. This is okay, and I get it—it must be strange to be a Korean living in India at an American school where your kid doesn't speak the same language as the teachers. But Maddie's PE teacher has a different spin on it: he openly and loudly refers to these students as the Korean Mafia.

Maddie—who has of course managed to break into a small subgroup of the Mafia and is learning Korean curse words in exchange for helping translate the teacher's instructions—once described the following scene, in which the whole PE class had to run a certain number of laps in a specific time frame to meet standards set in the state of Virginia, where the temperatures certainly do not reach India levels.

Maddie was running with a group of Korean boys. She happens to be taller and faster than they are, which isn't saying much, but it impressed the teacher. "Hey, you! Blondie! What's your name?" She answered him, and he immediately turned to the group of boys. "Listen up, Korean Mafia. This girl Maddie is beating you. That's embarrassing. And you, Chang, you run slower than my grandmother—and she's dead! Now, show some pride, for God's sake, and get up off the ground and run these laps! Move it!" This is apparently a fairly typical exchange, so no one said anything. Since this man is also the coach of the swim team, which Maddie is on, we are treated to his invectives on a daily basis.

"Mom, can we get a juice?" The kids like coming along to pick up Maddie because of the fresh juices made on-site at the Parent Association Store.

"A juice sounds nice, but we don't have much time today—so hurry, please. Boys, go get the juices while your sister and I load up," I reply. The boys scramble to the juice line, rupees jangling in their pockets, and I collect the backpacks and swim gear.

The little store, run by parent volunteers, preserves my sanity. I like the fact that once in a blue moon, I can get my hands on French bread—and once I really hit the jackpot and found a brick of imported English cheddar that no one had yet claimed. Shopping for food outside the local markets is a depressing endeavor because the many daily power outages around Chennai render the freezers nearly unusable; they are usually crusted over with juices and leakages from the meat and food's constantly defrosting and refreezing. The grocery store where we get the bulk of our dry goods is the local Amma Nanna chain, which is well known for bilking expats and foreign travelers by charging 1,000 rupees (approximately $20) for a damp, expired brick of Kraft cheese product. We grudgingly buy powdered formula at a whopping 3,500 rupees a can, because the first store I went to sold bags of pale yellow, still-warm milk and I decided then and there my formerly breastfed toddler was going to get formula after all. Our mainstay is fresh veggies and meats, which is a good thing anyway, but even if we wanted to eat like Americans, the prices for imported goods are prohibitive, and the offerings are invariably stale and past their shelf date.

The day I lucked out and stumbled upon that cheddar, it was like finding Willy Wonka's Golden Ticket. I had been craving the comfort of a nice midwestern casserole but had been hard-pressed to locate good cheddar cheese, which was the missing ingredient in a dish I longed for when homesick. On this auspicious day, I mixed the items into a near-perfect tuna noodle casserole and cooked them in a salvaged toaster oven from the storage room off the kitchen. Most Indian kitchens don't come with an oven, so my find was extra valuable, even if it worked only in ten-minute increments and had to be turned on with the help of a screwdriver.

Once it was done, I set it on the counter to cool but didn't count on how that would puzzle my cook. Lakshmain took one look at the melted mass in the glass dish, lifted it up and smelled it, and, before I knew what he was doing, promptly poured the contents into his dirty wok on the stovetop.

Lakshmain is very territorial about what goes on in his workspace. He is accustomed to working for women who grew up with staff and have zero interest in cooking or really even setting foot in "his" kitchen. Shemain has made certain I understand that my presence is always a mild affront to him, and I've made sure she and Lakshmain understood that, while I respect that, I am used to the kitchen being the heart of my home. I'm sure Lakshmain viewed the baked cheese dish as another sign of my foreign eccentricities and felt the need to remedy my culinary problem by adding curry and ghee and giving it a good toss in his wok, which I know for a fact has never been washed. My feelings were sharpened by homesickness, and I nearly cried.

"Why are we in such a rush today?" asks Maddie, who is still damp from swim practice, her cheeks flushed from exertion. It makes me happy to see her participating in school with such enthusiasm. Becoming a teenager is difficult, I know, but she is my first child and it saddens me to see the spark dulled in her as she sheds her childhood. I don't have older children to gauge her progress by, and so all I can do is hope for the best. The fact that India seems to be restoring some of her light is an unexpected gift.

I take her wet towel from her and answer as we walk. "Well, the car is full of art supplies, and I'm worried that the crayons are going to melt into one big mess before we get them home."

She flashes me a quick smile at the mention of the art supplies. "Are we really going to do my idea?" she asks. "The one we talked about the other day?" She takes a long pull from her juice, oblivious to the fact that her comment has caused my eyes to well up.

A few nights ago, she came into my bedroom and sat with me as I got ready for bed. Once I realized she wasn't in there to complain or tattle or ask me for something, I figured out that she just wanted to talk with me—just to be—and I couldn't remember the last time she had done that. When she was little, I couldn't keep her away from me—she would curl up on my lap like a mewling kitten and be her most charming self to avoid being sent to bed. Those shell-pink memories now seem like they happened a lifetime ago, and so I was stupidly grateful.

I watched her pick up a pair of earrings from my bedside table and hold them up to the light, tilting her head and squinting as she studied the rough-cut diamonds and small cabochon emeralds in a delicate gold setting. Bob found them at an antique shop in the Pondy Bazaar in T. Nagar. I love them because they are so exquisite and unique, but also because my husband stepped into a jewelry store without being dragged by the nose.

Maddie set them back on the table, where they connected with a gentle clink, and quietly addressed me. "Mom? Have you ever wondered how much good you could do if you bought food for the people in the slum on Anderson Road with the money it cost to buy these?" I sat there, stunned into silence. She continued, "I mean, they're so pretty and everything. But, I don't know. You have lots of jewelry already, and maybe it would be great if we could just spend our money on the people who don't have anything. I was actually kind of thinking that we could have the orphans make something, and then all of your friends back home could help, too. They could, like, buy the stuff the orphans made"—she gave me a sly look—"and those women have more jewelry than *you*."

I laughed as I regarded my teenage daughter. What got me was that she wasn't being snotty. Miles from snotty, in fact. She was being thoughtful and subdued and seemed genuinely interested in my answer. I looked into her wide green eyes and I just knew—I knew we were here to help and to do the little bit we could for the people around us. We weren't going to change the world, but I realized that, in waiting for something huge to happen, for our ability to execute a grand gesture, we were missing out on the smaller things that would at least change *us*. What was most stunning to me was that I hadn't come to this conclusion on my own—my teenage daughter, the one I'd nicknamed an ingrate, had done it for me.

I put my arm around Maddie's shoulders and give her a squeeze. "You bet we're doing your idea. I've cleaned the city out of art supplies, so there's no turning back now. Let's get a move on; we have a lot to do tomorrow."

We now average one or two visits to Teni and Silas's orphanage every week and have kept the pace for the past month or so. For the most part, we take it one day at a time. They are transparent about their needs, and we are transparent about how much we can help them. The positive part is that, outside of the big items —like cars, or houses in good neighborhoods—things here cost very little compared with prices in the States, so even on a budget, we are able to help these people in a way we all find meaningful. A sack of rice big enough to require two adults to carry it costs about the same as a regular-size package of gourmet rice from an American specialty store and can feed a large group for weeks.

Still, I never get over how shocking it is when I try to imagine subsisting like they do, one day at a time, hoping there is enough money for food, or clothes, or gas, or housing. But this is how

Teni and Silas live their lives. We have made small inroads in helping them in ways that will stay with them, such as going with them to open a checking account. Part of the reason they couldn't open one was the exorbitant opening balance required, and so Bob covered it, agreeing to do so as long as we got to disperse the initial funds ourselves, which we did.

At first it was overwhelming to hear our new friends' various spins on "God will provide," in light of the fact that they care for at least thirty children at a time. On the surface, such talk seemed irresponsible and cavalier. But I am not a woman who is tied deeply to a faith, like Teni and Silas are, and their commitment to the running of their nascent church is as strong as their commitment to the children. The church sits on the orphanage grounds and resembles a large steel shed, although they have installed a foundation and windows. The effort of growing a church and tending a congregation, as well as caring for the orphans, prohibits them from taking side jobs to supplement their income. As absurd as the business model seems, they have been doing it for over ten years, so we figure we are there not to rock their world, necessarily, but rather to be a thread in their life quilt, woven in at a time when they most needed it. They have managed to get some consistent help from local shop owners and members of their congregation, which is rather astounding when you figure in the monumental need that is present all around the city.

So I keep it simple and ask Teni for a list of what she needs, and it's never overwhelmingly large. However, they also need to start constructing a permanent building to house the girls on the small piece of property they own—because renting is cumbersome, always temporary, and too expensive over time.

I take the most recent list out of my purse:

Shoes for kids
New school uniforms for kids
Plastic mosquito netting for kids
Rice
School supplies
Used refrigerator

Chennai doesn't attract that many Westerners, so I really stand out and can't risk shopping on my own if I want to take advantage of the local prices. I usually bring Shemain with me when I shop to ensure that I get the best deals, with the added bonus that when I am with her, I never, ever have to pay additional money for delivery or any other small extras.

I was made aware of what a rarity we are in our section of the city when I exited the market with Shemain one day and saw a white man standing in the middle of the traffic meridian, looking lost. He was younger, with a backpack and a European air about him, and I couldn't stop staring—it had been so long since I had seen a white person outside my family or in the school that it felt strange spotting one in public. I poked Shemain in the shoulder and said, "Hey, look. A foreigner."

Saturday comes, and there is a cyclone outside. This isn't a figure of speech—we have quite literally had cyclone winds and monsoon rains for the past twelve hours. Now the weather has somewhat died down, although only a few hours ago, the fronds of our coconut tree looked as if an invisible hand were pulling them taut, so strong were the winds. When we ask Narynaan if he thinks it's wise to drive to the orphanage, he merely bobs his head from side to side and says, "No problem," reassuring us that the only time he hasn't been able to drive at all was during the recent tsunami.

I blithely sidestep the swiftly moving creek that formed overnight in our courtyard and bark orders at my family to help load up the car. I am happy about the project we have put together with Maddie's help, especially in light of what Teni and Silas have told us about the curriculum the orphans use. It is the goal of the orphanage that each child will learn a trade or skill that will put him or her into the marketplace and, eventually, solidly into the middle class. ("Middle-class" in India is a relatively new concept and includes a broader swath of criteria than it does in America. Shirmaly considers herself middle-class, although her family's income is less than $20,000 a year.)

Because Teni and Silas incorporate their religious beliefs into their daily lives, they are also working to equip all the children at the orphanage with a sense of empowerment and grace so that they will be able to help others once they are adults and no longer require assistance from others themselves. While Teni and Silas are certainly more right-wing in their Charismatic Christian beliefs than we are, their vision to support as many children as they can is something we can get behind.

Teni and Silas are also burdened with the job of saving for dowries for the older girls, who hope to make a decent marriage match while still under the care of the orphanage—and that's a catch-22 in many ways. Although the girls' socioeconomic situation severely limits what kind of match they can make, there is some wiggle room and possibility for upward mobility, and it all hinges on the size of their dowry. It makes no difference whether

JENNIFER HILLMAN-MAGNUSON

or not we agree with the concept, because it will happen with or without us, so we can choose to help or not. The arts, incidentally, do not register anywhere on the list of educational needs for the children, and that's what makes today special.

I watch Lakshmain and Rajaram lug over what looks like an enormous rolled carpet and load it into the back of the minivan. It barely fits; we will have to duck our heads on the long drive to the orphanage today.

Bob walks outside with the last bag of provisions. "Jen, what is that thing?" he asks.

"Remember? They needed mosquito netting for the windows. It was on their list," I answer. Admittedly, this doesn't look like the gauzy white netting thrown over a four-poster bed. It's a hideous, glue-colored plastic that is intended to be stapled or nailed to the walls. It's not attractive, but it's cheap, it keeps the disease-carrying mosquitoes out, and it's a viable alternative when there isn't money to pay for windows.

By the time we reach the orphanage, the rains have picked up again. The streets are filled with standing water, and while the roads aren't as congested with people and animals because of the pounding rain, they are literally clogged with debris, and parts of our route have taken on the appearance of a small river. There are no drains, so the water is left to stand and stagnate, and whatever trash or waste has accumulated on the ground floats on the newly formed brown rivers.

Friends of ours from the school tell us stories about the sinkholes that form on the coastal road leading from the school to the American enclave, and these nightmarish tales help validate our decision to live in the middle of the city—especially in light of newspaper stories detailing reports of missing persons who, it is later discovered, just fell into sinkholes and disappeared. As bizarre as this seems, it happens on a somewhat regular basis. Sound infrastructure is not something I ever thought I would be profoundly grateful for, but it is now, and I take unexpected comfort in the fact that my tax dollars back home just might be saving me from an obscure death should we ever have an epic storm.

We arrive at the orphanage to an extramuggy room, and there is a palpable feeling of restlessness in the air. I am impressed that the children aren't scaling the rooftops or wrestling with one another like energetic puppies, the way mine do the minute they decide they're "bored." Normally, a little rain doesn't stop these kids from kicking a ball around; we have played outside with them on the hottest days, as well as some fairly wet ones. Today, however, the field is temporarily a treacherous mud bog. I waver just a bit over our decision to spend the next several hours in such a sedentary project. When my own kids have been cooped up on a rainy day, the last thing they have wanted to do is sit still and paint or draw. They have invariably torn my house apart making cushion forts or constructing cities out of old boxes, or strewn every dress-up item they own around the room as they flit from one frenetic activity to another in an effort to burn off that enviable childhood energy. But then I remember that there are no couch cushions or empty boxes here, and I relax.

Maddie and Chloe get to work immediately and set up the plastic paint palettes, Jacob distributes the colored pencils, and Jack and I start cutting swaths of canvas to pass out to the kids. Henry chews contentedly on a paintbrush while Bob and Narynaan head over to the girls' new dormitory to install the mosquito netting. Bob accompanied Silas to tour a few prospective places and managed to negotiate a reasonable lease in a building with slightly better amenities than the last one.

I notice that the room is rapidly quieting down as everyone begins to inspect the art supplies in the box we've carried up from the car. Last week we brought an American football that was mailed to us from a friend in Oregon, and Bob and Jacob spent the afternoon going over the finer points of blocking and tackling with an eager crew of boys. I hope today's project isn't going to be a letdown. I am probably most excited about the tubes of oil paints and drawing supplies that I managed to find over the course of several excursions around the city. I'm especially proud because there are no Craft Warehouses or Michaels franchises, and hunting down anything in Chennai in the absence of GPS and reliable Internet is always a challenge. I perk up when I see one of the younger boys run his finger lightly over the bristles of an angled paintbrush. He's not fashioning it into a makeshift weapon and in fact seems genuinely curious, so I take that as my cue to get things rolling.

Something prompted me to pack our ancient art-supply tote, which has survived our many moves, road trips, and vacations over the years. I pull several large laminated cards from the bag and hold up a picture of Monet's pond. The room goes quiet—and, as always, I am impressed by the orphans' cooperation and attentiveness. I am a master of self-control as I resist the temptation to glare at my own kids and tell them *this* is how it's done, which really means only that I am absolutely no different from the generations of clueless parents who extol the virtues of disadvantaged children somewhere else in the world with the expectation that their own offspring will suddenly be hit with the clarity of how amazing their life is, relative to the rest of the world, and will promptly act like perfect human beings.

"Okay, you guys. It is *really* wet outside today. So we thought it would be fun to create our own masterpieces, like this one here. Does anyone know who painted this?"

The boy who was inspecting the paintbrushes raises his hand. "You, Auntie?"

Before I can respond, one of the older girls shoots him a look of disgust and raises her hand, looking pointedly at me for acknowledgment, and I nod my head. "It is from France," she answers, and gives the boy a withering look, to which he is apparently immune, as he sticks his tongue out at her.

"Yes! It is, and this artist painted his pictures in a really fun way, too," I pull out several other laminated reproductions and pass them around the room. "How do you feel about creating your own paintings today? You can paint absolutely anything you want. Or, if you would rather draw, I have pencils and crayons and pens as well." I look at the faces in the room and am buoyed by plenty of smiles.

Mithra raises her hand and points to the paintbrushes. "Auntie, you will need to show some of us how to use those."

Chloe grabs a few brushes and hands some to her sister while addressing the kids: "It's easy, and there's no wrong way, really. As long as you use colors you think are pretty and you're having fun, well, then you're doing it right." She addresses the room like a teacher, and I am proud of her initiative.

Everyone breaks off into groups of three to five, depending on the medium they want to work with. We get people set up with pencils, crayons, watercolors, oil paints, and markers. Chloe has taken over the groups that want to use pencils and watercolors, and I can hear her words of encouragement even over the din as she watches one of the boys draw. He looks Asian, and I know from Teni that his mother is a prostitute who likely conceived him with a tourist or foreign worker—they aren't entirely sure. I make my way over to him and peer over his shoulder to see what it is he is so diligently working on, and am surprised to see that he has already completed a simple pencil drawing of a bearded man and is going over the figure with watercolors. It is skillful and poignant, and I wonder who he is drawing and how he got so good.

I place my hand on his shoulder and lean in a bit. "That is a beautiful work of art. Truly, I can see this in a frame and on a wall." He ducks his head and keeps painting, but I can see a smile on his normally shy face. I am hit with inspiration and can't wait to get back home.

After our mini-art-fest, which goes on for nearly four hours, we have a small mountain of artwork from the kids. They have been prolific and have each produced at least several pieces, before finally tiring. We end the day with a modified game of Goat and Tiger, with indoor rules to preserve the adults' sanity, and we go home full with the happiness that comes from a productive day and the hope of something good around the corner.

That night, I sit at my computer and compose an e-mail to my entire neighborhood. I got the list from my friend, Nancy, who runs the e-mail communications for the gated community, and I know she has done me a huge favor by sharing it, given some of the high-profile people on it.

Hi, Neighbors,

Some of you may not know me, but I know Nancy has mentioned our absence in previous neighborhood correspondence. We are the family currently living in India (please contact me if anyone is having parties at my house!). As many of you know, we have made friends with a small local orphanage—and for those of you sending supplies, letters, and care packages, we are profoundly grateful! Attached are some gorgeous pictures—and there is a story behind each one. I'd like for you to each commit to purchasing one of these paintings or drawings (I will frame them once I'm back in America) to help raise money for these kids. I know many of you are used to giving at home, and there is always need wherever we go. But you are my neighbors and friends, and I'd like to exploit that fact to help these people who have come into our lives. So dig deep and shoot me an e-mail with your pledge, and I will send you a file with the painting you get. But, better than that, you get to be a small piece of their life, just like we are—and that's priceless.

Chloe and Maddie are looking over my shoulder as I type, and when I press SEND, I turn around and high-five my girls. "You guys are awesome." It's the best I have felt in years.

CHAPTER 11

We were told at our cultural sensitivity training that our adjustment to life in India would resemble an enormous roller coaster ride, filled with many "peaks and valleys." This is an understatement and a cliché, but true nonetheless. If I were teaching the class, I would just give it to them straight. I'd look the new couple from Des Moines right in their bloodshot eyes and tell them that in a few months they would be in Delhi, driving by a McDonald's, and at least one of them would burst into tears when they saw a sign for the McAloo Tikki, and that this would be normal, and in fact, hours later (after discovering that the McAloo Tikki isn't all that bad), they would be vowing to stay forever.

Bob's company sent us to this mandatory three-day seminar, where we were given the crib notes on how to behave in India, as well as helpful tips on what it is like to be a first-time expat. Of course, we took this class on our second day in India, after thirty hours of flying with the kids, complete with the massive, body-consuming jet lag that comes from crossing over twelve time zones in a day and a half.

Flying for me ceased long ago to be a glamorous endeavor. Bob, bless his heart, has the luxury of belonging to platinum or titanium, or whatever other trumped-up description of frequent-flier clubs applies to professionals. All this means is that he knows about warm towels in first class, not waiting in lines to check his luggage, and possibly watching sexy single travelers sneak into the first-class bathroom for their sexy single-people sex.

Not I. I will never be a part of a mile-high club or know what it is like to fly first class on an international flight, because I am too broke from the seven tickets we have to purchase at a time to get anywhere as a family unit, which is usually the only reason I am on an airplane in the first place. The only talents I have demonstrated in a plane bathroom at thirty thousand feet are an ability to use the toilet while taking a pull-up off a toddler and singing "The Itsy Bitsy Spider" over and over so said toddler doesn't cry or notice the fun blue water in the potty. It's not a skill set the sexy singles out there exactly covet. Subsequently, when we sat in the mandatory classes, I was cross-eyed with fatigue and remember only a few things, which means I may have failed India 101.

I do remember that it is important to take a business card with your right hand because the left hand has historically been used to wipe oneself in the bathroom in this part of the world. I know never to give a Hindu a gift made of leather (I name this the Holy Cow Rule so that I remember the part about cows being sacred). I have learned to wait for a man to shake my hand, because most likely he won't, and that offering my hand first would be considered downright brazen, if not rude.

But mostly I just remember the parts where they told us how we would likely feel as expats. They stressed over and over that our emotional adjustment to living here (as well as the adjustment to moving back home) would not be a linear progression. I have found absolute truth in this advice. One day I am up, up, *up*, and *Namaste, India! I love all of your pretty colors and nice people, and, my God, no one here says no; they just say "okay, okay" or "five minutes, madam," and boy, do I like that kind of positive thinking, and ooooh, is that butter chicken? And garlic naan? Yayyyyyy, India! I am going to save the world! And wear adorable tunics and bindis! I am one with the beauty of India. I'm like Julia Roberts in that movie! Ommmmmm.*

But the very next day I am inexplicably down, googling dengue fever after Jack wakes up spotted with too many mosquito bites to count and embarrassing myself when Shirmaly catches me telling an errant mosquito to "fuck off and die; I will kill your entire family if my baby gets sick," and by the time I am buying warm eggs at Amma Nanna and wondering why a country so filled with electricity and air conditioners still refuses to refrigerate anything, I realize I am *this close* to developing a raging case of Tourette's.

This lightbulb moment comes when I feel irrationally enraged at Narynaan when he inquires whether I'm okay and I tell him I have a headache. When I answer, it is to avoid a lengthy and personal explanation, and he responds that my headache is due to too much heat in my body from eating the wrong foods. I know Shemain is behind this statement, and I literally have to bite my tongue hard to stop myself from saying, "No, not really, Narynaan. It's actually just my superbloated uterus and the fact that I am likely bleeding right now on the backseat of your car. Bleeeeeding."

Peaks and valleys.

[*Gently smooths skirt.*]

Today I feel like I can do nothing right. I work for a little bit on some planning for the orphanage, but after my head threatens to rip itself off at the base of my skull and catch a plane back to America, where Target, Midol, and cabernet sauvignon are abundant, I give up the fight. I agree to let Jacob come with me to pick up Maddie from swim practice if he promises to be quiet (which is an enormous request for a boy who typically spends the *entire* forty-five-minute ride peppering me with questions, like how do I *really know* a pet monkey would be dangerous, if I've never had one; or what chemicals make the color green and also explode things; or how long is a light-year; or how much money would it cost to have a fish tank in your house that could hold a great white shark?).

Despite the blinding pain in my head, watching him try to keep his promise is comical. After a series of twitches, *murps*, and *eeps* and several minutes of seat kicking, I give in. "Jacob, do you need to tell me something? Can you please speak quietly, as Mommy has a really bad headache?"

He is like an overly inflated balloon releasing its air as he commences to tell me in rapid-fire speech about the multitude of things that have built up in his head in the span of no more than five minutes. "Mom, I hate to tell you this, because I know that you don't like motorcycles because they are dangerous, but I was thinking that if I am going to be the first Scientist of Everything, I am going to have to learn to ride one, because you can't always take a car into the jungle. And I will have to scuba dive. Oh, and if having a blue-spotted octopus as a pet is illegal—it is, look it up—what if you are a scientist and you just want to study it? For *science*?"

Peaks and valleys.

One of the downfalls of wanting to do as much as possible in a finite time frame, as happens here in India, is that sometimes I end up feeling like nothing is being done well. The concept of hyperspecializing in any one thing boggles my mind; there are just so many things out there to experience that I can't imagine ignoring most of them in order to understand everything about one or two areas in life. Now that Bob is quickly hitting his targets with his company's India team and I know our time in India is therefore drawing to a close, I feel a growing panic. Is Shemain right after all? Have we done everything wrong? What have we missed out on experiencing? Should we have stayed in an ashram? I know this is ridiculous—my kids are not going to do yoga for hours on end, then meditate, and then cap it all off with a dinner of lentils and jasmine tea. This doesn't stop me from becoming irrationally fixated on the things we could have done, though.

A friend of mine from the American school, Chauncy, asked my family to join hers on a camping trip in Kerala, a state in India to the west of us, bordering the Arabian Sea. Her son has come over several times to play with Jacob, and we have developed a routine after school as we wait for the older children to come out of class, where we talk while the other kids burn off some energy. I have shared some of Chauncy's stories with Bob, so when I mention the offer of camping near her hometown, he gives me a firm "no way" and reminds me of the coffee-bean-and-tiger story. Which, on reflection, is pretty reasonable.

Chauncy grew up in a large, poor family, but they lived well, since they were farmers, and at one point they grew coffee on their smallish plantation. I asked her what that was like, not only because I was curious but also because romantic visions of *Out of Africa* cloud my judgment about pretty much everything, so if I didn't clarify, I would have ended up picturing Chauncy as Meryl Streep in a gauzy dress, saving her coffee bean farm from ruin before submitting to the ravishing Robert Redford.

Chauncy shrugged off my question at first, saying it was the same as regular farming, except it took up more land and so they had to have extra cows on hand. Naturally, the extra cows came in handy. Whenever Chauncy or her brothers were required to tend the plants on the farthest edges of the farm, they would take a cow with them. The cow would then be tethered between the forest and the laboring child. This method ensured that when the tigers came out, as they apparently did with regularity, they would eat the cow and allow the child to get away.

I come to find out the campground Chauncy had in mind for us was made up of tree houses suspended thirty feet off the ground, partly to keep campers safe from tigers. Even though I know this is the last thing on Earth we should do with our kids, I still suffer a twinge of feeling like we are missing out.

Of course, I know that I get this way even more acutely when I am feeling down or, in this case, helpless. I just read an e-mail from Teni, and it has me in a funk of helplessness and overall sadness about the amount of need not only in the orphanage but all around us in India. Even if we had the luxury of unlimited funds, it feels like a black hole that will never be filled. In the e-mail, Teni went over the usual points she does when she corresponds with me—checking on our kids, giving me any small updates that have come up with the orphans, and touching base about their needs for the week. But this time, she made a point of asking me to make sure to bring my camera—which is an odd request, since I am never without it. She goes on to say that she wants me to look at Revathy's leg and take pictures so that Bob and I can "know what to do about it."

Revathy is a quiet, sweet girl of about twelve who doesn't say much, but she always comes to show me her work. Usually I am initially unaware of her presence, and then I realize that she has been sitting very close to me, often for some time, while I distractedly tend to Henry or Jack or talk with another child around me. Every once in a while, I'll feel her resting her hand on my arm or shoulder.

By the time our next visit rolls around, I am jumping out of my skin with anticipation of what is waiting for us. We pull up to the main building, and Teni motions me over while Bob and the kids go start a movie we have brought for the children. In a fit of nostalgia, we found a copy of *Finding Nemo* that we can project onto a sheet using our laptop. Teni takes me to the side of the building, where Revathy is sitting on a stone step. Revathy is wearing her usual orange top and long, matching skirt. She gives me a small smile and glances anxiously at Teni, and I see Teni offer her a small, reassuring nod.

Revathy reaches down and pulls up the hem of her skirt, and I feel the shock rip through me. One of her legs is a twisted mass from the midcalf down to the ankle. Her bone looks bent nearly in half, and the ravaged skin is puckered and weathered. Worse, just above her ankle is a large, maybe four-inch, circular, open wound. It isn't bleeding, and, amazingly, shows no sign of infection, but the exposed pink flesh is stark against the surrounding deep-brown skin.

I open my mouth to speak but realize I don't know what to say, much less do. I bend down in the dirt and rest on my heels, and rub my temples for a moment while I collect myself. "Oh, Revathy. Honey. Does it hurt?"

She gives a slight bob of her head. "When I walk, Auntie."

I look at Teni. "When did this happen? *What* happened?"

Teni helps Revathy with her skirt and answers me in her singsong voice. "Well, we are not sure, yes? Revathy has been with us for six or seven months, and her leg was like this when she came here. It could be a snakebite, or she could have fallen off a motorbike." She bobs her head again from side to side and fixes me with a steady look. I am aware of a mounting pressure in my chest so hard I worry if I'm having a panic attack. I need to get Bob over here, I realize, but I am still immobile with disbelief. We aren't doctors. And they have let this poor girl live with this wound and deformity for at least half a year. *Half a year.* I am glad to be sitting, because I feel like I have been hit in the face with a bag full of bricks. I also know Teni well enough by now to understand that this is her way of saying that unless we intervene, Revathy will live with this in perpetuity—that is, if it doesn't kill her or further deform her.

For the first time, I am filled with anger at this woman's assumptions. And I also have to hand it to her—she knew the entire time about Revathy's leg yet chose to say nothing until now. And now we are connected to each child in this orphanage; we have incorporated all of them into our life routine; our commitment is obvious. Teni must know this. For a brief moment, I want to unleash my sarcasm and give her a "well played" to let her know I am onto her, but I recognize the futility in doing so and bite my tongue. Instead, I say only, "I am going to go get Bob."

My husband is the person you need when you are panicked or need to get something done that no one else will touch because it is a monumental hassle. He is the man you need in situations like this. Where I am prone to giving in to the kind of knee-jerk emotional responses that usually yield less-than-satisfactory outcomes, Bob takes his time, thinks through every angle, and gets results.

I know that Revathy's leg bothers him deeply when he sees it for himself, but he doesn't say much about it at first. He listens to my rant all the way home about how helpless I feel, how angry I am at Teni and Silas for not telling us—how infuriated in general I am at the entire overwhelming reality of children in poverty in India—and then merely hugs me and says quietly, "Jen, why don't you let me handle this one?"

Several days later, he tells me he is driving to Apollo Healthcare to meet with the CEO. This news makes me nervous. "Bob, remember the ER doc at the Apollo clinic? Are we sure this is the place to go?" I had a run-in with Apollo Health recently when a doctor there hastily prescribed an indeterminate medication for Henry after he had a scary reaction to a mosquito bite, and while everything turned out fine, I remain less than impressed.

It turns out that the meeting with the Apollo CEO is a good place to start but ultimately not productive. He agrees to talk with Bob ostensibly because of professional courtesy, but that's about it. The CEO is friendly, full of smiles and head bobs, but at the end of the day he is noncommittal—in other words, a classic bureaucrat. Bob's next stop is with a family practitioner at Apollo Health, who is slightly more helpful and sets Bob up with a friend of his, an orthopedic surgeon, in the same hospital. Bob takes the meeting, and that's where he strikes pay dirt.

Dr. Singh is Indian but has family in Atlanta, Georgia. He and Bob hit it off from the start—Bob says the minute they begin their small talk, he could tell this man was thoughtful and compassionate. After a long initial conversation about Revathy's wounds and our desire to see her better, he asks my husband straight out, "Why are you doing this?"

Bob replies simply, "Because it is the right thing to do."

Dr. Singh takes this in and then says, while looking at Bob, his hands folded in front of his face, "It is just very strange to me. There are so many people in India who have the means to help. And yet you are a foreigner and here you are, shuttling this girl, a stranger, through our health care system for no real reason that I can see." At this point, Bob thinks he has lost Dr. Singh, but then he continues, "As doctors, we wouldn't be doing our fair share if we didn't waive our fee. I will talk to the plastic surgeon I work with and see if he will do the same."

This is his way of saying he will fix Revathy's leg and arrange for discounts or free medical care along the way as he can. And so the surgery to fix Revathy's leg is arranged.

Bob takes this on as his own project. He meets with Teni and Revathy five or six different times for doctor's appointments, to get X-rays and MRIs, or to give blood for lab work, and decides he will go to the hospital to be with Revathy on the day her nine-hour surgery is scheduled. Revathy, while still as quiet and reserved as ever, holds Bob's hand while crossing the street to the hospital and sits near him during the many meetings and appointments leading up to her surgery.

Seeing my husband take time away from the demands of his job, not to mention the demands of all of us at home, helps me see him in a new light. It's crucial to surprise your partner, no matter how long you've been together, and I admit I thought I had Bob down pat. I didn't—and this tender side of him for someone outside our family underscores why I married him in the first place.

One wrinkle we haven't anticipated is our timeline in India. By the time Bob gets Revathy's surgeries scheduled and coordinated, we are looking down the barrel of our move back to the States. We are all there for Revathy while she endures her painful skin graft and the subsequent recovery time, but our return is inevitable, so Bob ends up scheduling flights home for me and the four younger kids, and he and Maddie agree to stay behind to wrap up work and school and to see Revathy through the final stage of her surgery.

The morning of her procedure, Revathy is terrified. Bob writes me that she cried all the way to the hospital, and she was so distraught that the surgeon eventually asked Bob if he wouldn't mind rolling her into surgery. Revathy had asked for him. He did, and by the time the anesthesia took effect he was a wreck—but he didn't call me, because it was the middle of the night in America.

Back in Tennessee, I wake up from a dream so crystal clear it feels as if it actually took place. In it, I could see Revathy, and while she said nothing, her faced glowed with peace, and she smiled at me. She then lifted the hem of her skirt to show me her leg, which was as smooth and clear as her other one. I reached out to her, but she was gone.

As I awaken, I lie in bed with a profound sense of well-being. Logically, I tell myself that I dreamed this because I knew she was heading into surgery. But in my heart, I want to think that Revathy understood her connection to our family and communicated to me during her operation. I want to think that she was letting me know she was going to be okay—which she was, and still is. The feeling of peace that I have is real and lasting—a gift we are given when we have the honor of getting outside ourselves and helping where it doesn't make any sense.

CHAPTER 12

Too soon, we are faced with the reality that we have to move back home to Nashville. Now that the countdown to our departure has begun, time decides to speed up to a decidedly American pace as we try to cram our final moments with as many memorable experiences as possible, chief of which is attending an Indian wedding—an item on my bucket list that I didn't think would receive the satisfactory check of completion, since it requires knowing two locals who are planning their ceremony while we are still living in Chennai.

Shemain, of course, is quite familiar with my list and has told me that even if we manage to befriend a couple in time, it is doubtful that we will be invited, because we are foreigners. So I am gleeful the day Bob comes home from work with a wedding invitation from one of his coworkers, and I promptly wave this proof of my good fortune in Shemain's face. She looks it over and

comments only that the event is a mere two days long—
impressive to me, but apparently "proper" festivities would last a
week or more and would be filled with lavish touches, such as the
wedding party's arriving on elephants. Clearly, we have been
invited to a subpar wedding, she sniffs.

I don't care. I am already hit with partial amnesia over any
struggles I have endured—missing home, missing my family,
missing my village. Now, I am like a woman on her final days of a
family vacation, trying to soak up the last sunsets and carefree
moments in an effort to turn feelings of happiness into a tangible
thing. I wish I had understood this when buying souvenirs—that
doing so is really the search for a placeholder, a physical reminder
of when we felt joyous.

During our last week, Shirmaly asks us to a farewell dinner at
her home. She lives across the city in a tightly packed
neighborhood of cinder-block buildings that feels vaguely like
old-school Harlem or Queens, only with dirt roads and more
clotheslines hanging out the windows. We make our way upstairs
to the third-floor apartment, and a proud Shirmaly gives us a tour.
She and her husband live with their two children and his mother.
The front door opens onto a small living area containing a couch
and a chair and a small computer desk. They have set up a
makeshift table with a checkered cloth for our dinner, and a few
items are placed neatly on the walls.

I take in the brass-framed mirror and a small flower print, and
then I balk but try to recover quickly so I don't embarrass myself,
or Shirmaly. Right in the middle of the wall above the brocade
couch is a picture of our family, taken at the beach. I'm sure she
put it there in honor of our visit, but the gesture seems almost too
big—and I don't want to impart how self-conscious it makes me

feel. Even though I understand the strict social hierarchies that are present in this culture, I do not accept that money or birth circumstances make one person better than another, but I don't want to inadvertently insult Shirmaly's sweet intentions, either.

Jack points and says, "Hey, that's me!"

I shuttle him toward the kitchen and nod, then look over at Shirmaly's mother-in-law, who is right next to us, and smile. "Yes, it is. How lucky are we to have our picture at Shirmaly's house?" I keep moving. The kitchen is separated from the front room by a pale-pink-and-white floral curtain that has been pulled back to reveal a small but neat and functional Indian kitchen. Whatever Shirmaly is cooking smells heavenly, and I want to linger and take in the savory goodness wafting through the air.

We turn around, and Shirmaly points to two small rooms with their doors open and beds inside, and that concludes our tour. All in all, it is a tiny but absolutely charming apartment. I do manage a quick prayer of thanks that living with one's in-laws isn't a cultural requirement in my home country.

In typical Indian fashion, we are served first, as the guests of honor, and the meal makes me want to cry. Shirmaly has obviously taken note of our favorite foods over the months of working with us, and every single one is present at dinner. We love fish, and she has made at least four different curried varieties, which she ladles up and pours over fluffy mounds of jasmine rice. There is sambar and dal, and piles of buttery naan bread on a plate in the middle of the table. She has made mutton for Bob, and a gorgeous platter of chicken *biryani*. I can't imagine what her market bill must have cost her, and my throat is thick with gratitude. We eat until we feel ill.

After dinner, we follow Shirmaly's children downstairs to the street below. There are no streetlights, but light from the surrounding apartments allows us to see well enough. As if on cue, several children and their families exit their homes, and before we know it, the street is crowded with people. Shirmaly introduces us to her neighbors, and I see that her son has run upstairs and is now back with a well-worn cricket bat in his hands. Within minutes we are all lined up, taking turns to play an impromptu game. I am wearing heels, since I dressed up out of respect for the occasion, and I can't believe myself—former germaphobe that I am—as I slip my shoes off and throw them to the side of the road when it is my turn to bat. I am having so much fun my cheeks hurt, and Bob and my kids are obviously enjoying themselves as much as I am. It's a giddy feeling, this synchronization of well-being among all seven of us. I feel like the luckiest woman on the planet.

If you had asked me a year ago if I would be having the time of my life on a dirty, unpaved street, playing a ball game with people I don't know in a run-down urban neighborhood, I can't imagine how confused I would have been. Now, it just seems like the most logical and beautiful thing in the world.

Not to be outdone, Narynaan also invites us over for dinner. The day we drive to his parents' home in the country, close to the orphanage, is an unusually hot and dry one, lacking the typical mugginess. Their neighborhood is peppered with brightly colored row houses, painted in apricots and purples, blues and burgundies. The street dead-ends at a small temple roughly the same size as the nearby residences, its religious identity made obvious by the totems flanking the doors, piled high with various gods and goddesses painted in vivid shellac.

Narynaan's entire family appears to have shown up for this dinner. In addition to his parents, we meet his brother, sister-in-law, and several cousins. The men are buttoned up in shirtsleeves, and the women are all in a rainbow of saris. It is instantly apparent that this is to be a more formal dinner than we had at Shirmaly's, and the room crackles with nervous energy. I suspect this formality stems from the mere fact that Narynaan is not a part of our lives in the intimate way Shirmaly is, and he subsequently puts us on an even taller pedestal than she does. Despite Shirmaly's view of our family as "higher" socially, she has nonetheless witnessed us at our most vulnerable—whether that means domestic bickering or diaper changes or the countless unguarded moments that happen inside the sanctity of home.

Luckily, Bob picks up on this and moves to shake Narynaan's father's hand and break the ice with an impromptu statement: "Sir, it is an honor to finally meet your family. We have been so fortunate to have your son as our driver." He turns and clasps Narynaan on the shoulder as he speaks. "I am very protective of my family, and India is much different than America. Narynaan has kept me and my family safe while we have lived here, and we are forever grateful. He is a fine young man, and you have done an excellent job as parents."

I know Narynaan well enough by now to see that he is a little taken aback but also pleased by the praise. Bob is spot-on, of course. We could have been killed a dozen different times if it weren't for Narynaan's skillful knowledge of the lay of the land where we are merely long-term tourists.

Bob's words have the desired effect—Narynaan has made his

family proud—and also set the tone for the rest of our dinner. I am thankful to see that everyone appears more relaxed, and the room feels more convivial than when we first walked in. I take a seat on one of two large couches, and Narynaan's mom brings out a painted tray and presents it to me and the children. Resting artfully on two shiny green banana leaves is a small pile of Twix candy bars.

I shoot Narynaan a grin. "You remembered these are the kids' favorite!" The boys immediately reach for the candy, unaware of the thought that went into the purchase. As far as I know, only a few shops in the city sell the American candy bars, and whenever we have visited Oxford Book and Supply Store, whichever kid has been with me has always left clutching a Twix bar. Narynaan must have noticed this and told his parents. I think of all the care the people who work with us have devoted to these meals we are sharing with them, and it is almost too much; my cup runneth over.

Instead of serving us first and then joining in, Narynaan's entire family places food on the table in front of us and stands around the table to watch us eat—for the entire meal. It feels disconcerting, but by now we have experienced that sensation enough in India to just roll with it. After we finish, Narynaan asks if we want to go in the back and see the banana trees. Jacob and Jack leap up and scramble after him. Jacob lets out a whoop, and I can tell he needs to get outside after being closely observed during dinner. Bob and I take our time following the rest of the family out to the yard.

"We get our banana leaves for special dinners from these trees," Narynaan points out with pride. I nod; they really are impressive-looking. They take up nearly the entire enclosed space, and a large, red, conical flower dangles from one of them. Jacob is already underneath it, poking around, while Jack is jumping and missing, trying to dislodge the hanging flower with a stick.

Narynaan calls out to the boys, "Jacob! You brave boy! Find the cobras! They live in the banana trees!" He laughs, and the men around him chortle as well as he turns to them and says something in Tamil. I give him my best stern-mother look. "Not funny, Narynaan. If there were really cobras here, we would be in the car," I joke back.

A puzzled look crosses his face. "Madam, truly. We have two cobras who live with us. They are gods."

My body goes cold for a split second, and I mentally calculate how far we are from the nearest hospital—which, by my estimate, is nearly an hour's drive. "Boys! Get over here right now!" My voice sounds shrill, and I wonder if it will rouse the snakes—or hopefully repel them. I cross the yard in a few large steps and grab my sons, lifting one under each of my arms while I walk toward the back door of the house.

My legs start to shake as the adrenaline rush wears off. "Narynaan, you should have told me there were cobras in your backyard before you let the boys play." I am panting, aware that everyone is listening intently to me. I try to modulate my voice so I won't embarrass him. "If they had been bitten, they would be dead before we could get them to a hospital."

Now he looks even more confused, and I can see my tone has stung him. He starts bobbing his head and stuttering: "Madam, they would not bite the boys. We give them a chicken egg each morning as an offering."

It is hard for me to stay angry at him, especially since the boys are fine and I don't think I can explain to him that the agreement he and his family have entered into with the resident cobras isn't exactly an ironclad contract. My lips press together, resigned. "Okay, Narynaan. But my boys do not live here, and your snakes don't know them. So, to be safe, we are going to go back inside, okay?"

In spite of Shemain's protestations that the wedding to which we are invited is destined to be lackluster, it is a magical experience for Bob and me, filled with colors and sounds and customs we have never experienced. The ceremony takes place at a temple we have noticed before; we are excited to finally step inside the riot of colors and jumble of deities that catch our eye each time we drive past it.

Hindu gods and goddesses drape themselves over every square inch of the temple's exterior; a pensive green Lord Hanuman, a regal white-and-gold Krishna, the goddess Shiva, with her Mona Lisa smile, all tumble together as we pose for a picture underneath them in an archway, proud in our new clothes. Over his dress pants, Bob has on a white kurta—a long tunic with a mandarin collar that reaches to his knees. I am also wearing a kurta, which I have paired with leggings, but mine is stiff with elaborate colored embroidery and glints satisfactorily in the sunshine whenever the beading catches the light.

At the entrance, a temple worker pauses from her work of breaking off small bits of holy *tulsi* leaf in a large woven basket to take our shoes, which I surrender with more than a little trepidation as she tosses my favorite Banana Republic strappy sandals into a pile of several dozen worn slippers.

Once inside, we are led to our chairs in the ceremony room.

The seats are arranged in a circular fashion around the center of the room, which is partially indoors and partially exposed to a courtyard. In the middle are a holy man, the bride and groom, and about a half dozen other people sitting around a small fire, which occasionally flares up as the priest tosses in bits of leaves, powders, and oil. A distant relative of the bride's sits to my right and leans in periodically to help me understand the significance of what is happening. "He is pouring ghee onto the fire so that they may have abundance in their life together," she whispers into my ear. When it becomes obvious that the bride's family is going to sit through the ceremony with stoic faces, compared with the easy smiles coming from the groom's side, the relative observes that her family is none too pleased with the match, as it wasn't properly arranged and, rumor has it, they already live together. I nod and keep quiet. I already know from Bob that the couple has shared an apartment since they met at work over a year earlier.

At one point, an elderly woman comes around, carrying a large bowl filled with a sticky yellow substance. She scoops up a small bit with her fingers and hand-feeds it to each guest, as with church Communion. When it is my turn, I have already watched half of the room eat from her hands, before she places the food back into the bowl to reform a ball. Auntie must sense my trepidation, because she tells me it would be dishonorable to refuse the offering, called *ladoo*: saffron, wheat, sugar, and cardamom. So I try my best not to look uptight as I scrape the cloyingly sweet concoction from her fingers with my teeth, and I focus instead on the thrill of engaging in something so new to my senses.

After a few hours, we return home, and the next day Bob and I make an appearance at the reception. Contrary to Shemain's opinion, we find it quite similar to any other after-party and spend the evening stuffing ourselves with richly seasoned offerings and dancing around a large swimming pool. No elephants needed—I am content to have the experience.

"Shemain, I know they're just string, but you're buying one anyway. Wait, never mind one—you're buying ten." I hold a box filled with vibrant-hued string bracelets woven with beads. They look a lot like elaborate friendship bracelets, and the kids at the orphanage spent several days making them, after Maddie and Chloe gave them a tutorial. It was another idea the girls came up with to help find creative, albeit small, ways to earn some money.

"You are charging people money for these?" Shemain asks with an arch of her brow, holding up one of my favorite ones by a lone thread.

I snatch it back and put it in the box with the others. "Yes," I say pointedly. "They're adorable, they were cheap to make, and kids back in the States are really into this kind of thing." I give her my best exaggerated, Shemain-esque eye roll. "I don't care whether or not you wear them, but you're going to buy them." I'm suddenly inspired, as all of my dealings with Shemain have taught me well. I give her a look. "Just do it, okay, Shemain?" I finish with the most dramatic head bob I can muster.

She laughs, grudgingly opens her bag, removes several bills, and hands them to me. I move to take them, but for a moment she doesn't let go. "If you aren't careful, you will swiftly become taken advantage of here. Not everyone is as honest as they seem." She releases the money, and I put it in the box.

I know she is looking out for us. And I know she is right, as I think back to Teni and Silas purposely holding out on us about the state of Revathy's health. Surprisingly, even armed with this knowledge, I don't care. If we are essentially overcharged in the course of helping, then so be it. We are helping anyway, and it feels good.

I look at Shemain and, on impulse, take her face softly with my hands. Before she can protest, I kiss her cheek. "I love you, Shemain. I'm glad you worry about how wrong we are doing things here."

She blinks at me a few times, and I'm surprised to realize that she is about to cry. She takes my hands and places them in hers, then clears her throat. "Well, I suppose now is as good a time as any . . . Wait here a moment," she says, and she heads outside.

When she comes back in, she is holding a large, flat package. It's maybe four feet by three feet and wrapped in plain brown paper. She sets it on the table and looks at me. "Jennifer, your staff will give you cards and pictures of themselves to remember them by. That is fine. But I am not your staff." She pushes slightly at the package. "I want you to have this, so that you might remember me." I am so in the moment, so thrown by her touching gesture, that I don't immediately make a move to open my gift. She lets out an exacerbated sigh. "Jennifer, go. Open it."

I peel back the paper and see that it is a painting of some sort. "Oh, Shemain, you shouldn't have. I am so excited to see what this . . ." I don't finish, because as I turn the stretched canvas over to the front side, I see that she has gifted me an enormous oil painting—of herself. I run my fingers over the dried paint, over Shemain—larger than life, wearing a sari, her hair pulled back and a ruby bindi in the middle of her forehead. She is gazing ahead in her classic stare, her form partially concealed by a large palm frond. I'm both delighted and amused. "Shemain, this is fabulous. You know I will have to hang this above my bed," I joke.

She pauses a moment. "Yes, of course you will."

Something our cultural assimilation class briefly touched on was that our reentry into life in the United States would be just as fraught with emotional ups and downs as learning how to be an expat in India. At the time, I scoffed. Really? Adjusting to life with clean water? Easily accessible and plentiful food? Everything I need at the touch of a button or a short drive to the mall? Clean floors with no bugs or deadly diseases being tracked in? Sounds terrible. As in, *Look at that terrible mountain of cash with my name on it.* Please.

Now, many months later, I am back home. For the past week, I have alternated between acting like a sanctimonious jerk, like a weepy sentimentalist, or as if I never left India in the first place.

We attended Chloe's choir performance just a couple of weeks after we got home—I thought it was best to just put the kids back in school as soon as possible, and, after a week of falling asleep in class because of jet lag, they were fine. It was a delightful evening, with the kids from her junior high reenacting a royal feast from the 16th century. The families were seated at banquet tables, and we were served a meal that consisted of a whole turkey leg, roasted potatoes, and steamed peas and carrots.

I overheard a comment from a young girl at our table as she complained to her mother, "Gross! This doesn't even *look* like real food!"

I felt my sphincter close and my spine straighten as I willed myself not to so much as look her way. The words I wanted to say burned hot on my tongue. *Maybe it doesn't look like real food to you because you have been raised on a steady diet of preformed and pressed "chicken" shapes and snacks in tubes. Let's grab your mom and dad and go on a Jamie Oliver marathon and learn what those green and orange things on your plate are called, mmmkay? Do you have any concept of how lucky you are? How that plate of food would feed a family of four in India?*

I finally allowed myself a glance at the offender, someone I wanted desperately to throttle. She was an adorable girl of maybe nine or ten. Clearly, she just hadn't recently come home from living in the third world. I put my head down on the school table and chided myself for being an asshole.

Then, just a few days later, I was standing in line at my local Starbucks. Two young men were ahead of me, engrossed in conversation. They looked Indian—thin, shirts neatly tucked in— and one of them was wearing socks and flip-flops, which were notable mainly because it was snowing outside. But it wasn't until I saw the trademark head bob that my heart skipped a beat.

I interrupted their conversation: "Excuse me. Where are you from?"

They abruptly stopped speaking. "Uh, Nashville," one said.

"No, I mean *originally.*"

They shot each other a glance, the kind you might give your companion when approached by a bag lady raving about the talking cabbage people who live in the sewers and have stolen your dog.

"India."

The rainbows and sunbeams practically shot out of me as I

gushed, "I just got back from there!" My eyes welled up with tears. *Brethren! Maybe I should tell them how my baby still calls for Lakshmain in Hindi. Maybe they know how to make the carrot dish that we used to eat all the time but that I can't manage to prepare properly.*

One of the men said something to his friend in a dialect I didn't recognize. "Uh, great. Welcome back." They turned and resumed their conversation, and I wiped away the tear meandering down my cheek.

And finally, one day when I was navigating Nashville traffic in our packed-to-the-gills minivan, I forgot everything I had thought, mentioned, or vowed in India. I thumped the steering wheel and snapped peevishly at my husband, "Our kids are getting bigger than we are! I need a Suburban if I'm going to maintain my sanity chauffeuring these kids around for the rest of my adult life." I jabbed angrily at the air and shifted my weight in my heated leather seat. "Seriously, Bob. This is a total nightmare!"

To my credit, I have to say that my readjustment to America was made slightly worse by the amoeba that I picked up somewhere in India. I suspect it might have been the beautiful street food I ate while traveling with Shemain, although honestly, I could have gotten it anywhere. The effects of the parasite living in my body didn't show up right away. Initially, I was tired. Well, I had jet lag and was parenting four of the kids by myself while Bob and Maddie finished up business in India. Then I started losing weight. What American woman in her right mind is going to question weight loss? The first time someone mentioned how thin I was getting, I simply smugly credited my simpler life habits and *real* yoga.

One day I walked into my country club, a good fifteen

pounds lighter, my skin tinged a pale yellow, the cords on my neck sticking out a little too prominently. I looked terrible and years older and felt vaguely sick all the time, but my girlfriends took one glance at me and gushed, "Oh my *God*, Jen, you look amazing!"

After I was hospitalized and treated, some of my friends still joked that they wished they, too, were amoeba-thin. Sadly, once all of my foreign visitors were expelled from my GI tract, I promptly gained the weight back.

It isn't until now, about two months after our return, that I feel we have come full circle.

"Ingrates!"

It is after school, and we are all gathered in the kitchen, almost as if the past year didn't happen. The girls' heads are bent over their phones, issuing rapid-fire thumb texts with an intensity I know their schoolwork doesn't receive. The boys have thrown their backpacks down in the middle of the floor and are in the pantry, rummaging for after-school sustenance. It feels surreal to contemplate that just a few weeks ago, our pantry was an off-limits place, filled with storage and mosquitoes. I'm making grilled cheeses for the kids without a second thought to the fact that we didn't eat a single cheese sandwich while in India. I made the beds this morning, drove the kids to school, and entertained Henry while printing out my already packed to-do list. Life, it seems, is back to normal.

"Ingrates! Come over here." I place the sandwiches on plates.

They peel themselves off the couch and lumber to the counter with exaggerated effort, lest I forget how difficult it is for children to initiate movement in the hours after school. They tuck into their grilled cheese, and I give them all a smile. The last time I remember doing this, I read them an article about a perfect stranger and expected them to feel immediate inspiration, like I did.

I poke at the local newspaper in my hand to get their attention. Then I poke once more for good measure. "Hey, I want to read something to you guys." Maddie and Chloe both shoot me a wary look. "No, really. It's okay. It's an article about a local family who went and had an adventure and came back with some pretty inspiring stories."

I turn the paper to face them so they can all see their picture on the front page. A week ago, a journalist came to the house to interview us for a color piece on our time in India. The article features a photo of Maddie, Chloe, and Jacob with several of the boys from the orphanage—and they all have huge smiles on their faces.

I read: "'My favorite thing about living in India was how much we got to help other people,' said Jacob Magnuson."

I put the paper down on the counter and look at my children. "You know what? I'm really heartened by these kids. I think we should all do something about it."

"Mom!" Chloe groans, but she is grinning. I look around the room. They all are. And I have to say, that's inspiration enough.

While we lived in India for less than a year, it deeply impacted all of us in ways that were both good and bad and sometimes totally surprising. I wish I could say we came back with a passel of adopted children, but we didn't. I already have a passel, and mine don't listen when I tell them we need to downsize to make room for more. We didn't give up life in America forever so that we could call India home and change the world one small orphanage at a time. And while we did indeed raise quite a bit of money for the orphanage, we did not have enough funds in the end to build entirely new sleeping quarters and a school.

That said, we did learn. When we first got back at the end of 2010, we came home with experiences that had left an indelible imprint on our family and within our hearts. We made enough of a dent in the needs of the orphanage that it kept on surviving and is now breaking ground on a new building. We learned what it feels like as a family unit to be a part of something bigger than we are, and that the biggest changes we can make are the small ones right where we happen to be—no exotic location necessary. As the indomitable Mother Teresa said, "If you can't feed a hundred people, just feed one." I was in need of a wake-up call to this truth. India showed me that really, none of us really needs India to understand this.

We continue our quest for development and growth as a family, and, like the children of God that we are, we make mistakes and have setbacks along the way, but we get back up, brush ourselves off, and continue learning. We took an afternoon class to help with our reassimilation, which also served to highlight how much we and our priorities had changed.

The moment we were back on American soil, my kids were full of wonder and observation about everything we had once taken for granted.

"Mom, the streets are so clean!" Jacob said on the airport shuttle home.

"Our house. It's so . . . big," Maddie said later that day as she emerged from the rec room upstairs. Her tone wasn't that of a girl impressed with her digs—she sounded lost. In fact, the cultural jolt she experienced after India was one from which she never fully recovered. Life in an affluent Southern town never fit her the same afterward, and she wilted inside while trying to regain the peace she'd felt in India. Less than a year after our return to Nashville, when we received news that we were being considered for a transfer to the Middle East, I jumped at the opportunity before the words *Abu Dhabi* were past my husband's lips.

Now, after two years in Abu Dhabi, we are once again living in the United States. We keep in regular contact with Teni, Silas, and the children at the orphanage.

ACKNOWLEDGMENTS

I have so many people to thank for helping make *Peanut Butter and Naan* more than just a series of fun stories to tell at cocktail parties. Initial thanks go to my literary agents, Danielle Miller and Joanna Mackenzie at Browne and Miller, for seeing that this could become a book in the first place.

To all of our friends in India and those who briefly crossed our paths but will remain forever in our hearts, I am eternally grateful—especially for Shemain, without whom our experiences in India would definitely have been "all wrong" and my stories would have been less interesting.

To Teni, Silas, and all of the beautiful children they care for, thank you for allowing us to be a part of your lives.

To my girlfriends in Tennessee and across the country, thank you for your support and friendship when I was living on the other side of the world. We are honored by each person who bought a painting to support the orphanage. A special thank-you to Nancy Post for spreading the word to so many on our behalf and securing much-needed funds for the kids there.

Thank you to my sweet, crazy, one-of-a-kind children, who allow me to write about them, who tolerate many consecutive dinners of frozen pizzas while I hide in my office and write, and who have an amazing ability to adapt to new cultures around the world. I love you, Maddie, Chloe, Jacob, Jack, and Henry.

Thank you to Annie Tucker for her extraordinary editing skills. Without her encouragement and ability to see structure where I saw only words, this book would still be languishing in my computer. Thank you to Brooke Warner and the team at She Writes Press—an innovative and amazing group of women who are changing the face of publishing. I am honored to be a part of this wave of change in the industry, especially one that propels our voices to center stage.

And finally, to my husband, Bob. No words suffice, but your belief in me has been a light in many dark moments when I wanted to give up. I will always love you.

ABOUT THE AUTHOR

Jennifer Hillman-Magnuson is a writer, reformed volunteer, and mom to five amazing kids. Her work has appeared in various print and online publications, including *Brain, Child* magazine, *Bitch* magazine, *The Imperfect Parent, mamazine,* and many others. She also wrote for Nickelodeon's first parenting website, Parents Connect, and is working on her second book, *Rag Doll.* She's lived all over the United States as an Air Force wife, and in two countries and the Deep South as a civilian. She now lives with her husband and children in Oregon, where they still dream of Indian food.

SELECTED TITLES FROM SHE WRITES PRESS

She Writes Press is an independent publishing company
founded to serve women writers everywhere.
Visit us at www.shewritespress.com.

Flip-Flops After Fifty: And Other Thoughts on Aging I Remembered to Write Down by Cindy Eastman. $16.95, 978-1-938314-68-1. A collection of frank and funny essays about turning fifty—and all the emotional ups and downs that come with it.

Daring to Date Again: A Memoir by Ann Anderson Evans. $16.95, 978-1-63152-909-2. A hilarious, no-holds-barred memoir about a legal secretary turned professor who dives back into the dating pool headfirst after twelve years of celibacy.

Seeing Red: A Woman's Quest for Truth, Power, and the Sacred by Lone Morch. $16.95, 978-1-938314-12-4. One woman's journey over inner and outer mountains—a quest that takes her to the holy Mt. Kailas in Tibet, through a seven-year marriage, and into the arms of the fierce goddess Kali, where she discovers her powerful, feminine self.

Seasons Among the Vines: Life Lessons from the California Wine Country and Paris by Paula Moulton. $16.95, 978-1-938314-16-2. New advice on wine making, tasting, and food pairing—along with a spirited account of the author's experiences in Le Cordon Bleu's pilot wine program—make this second edition even better than the first.

Splitting the Difference: A Heart-Shaped Memoir by Tré Miller-Rodríguez. $19.95, 978-1-938314-20-9. When 34-year-old Tré Miller-Rodríguez's husband dies suddenly from a heart attack, her grief sends her on an unexpected journey that culminates in a reunion with the biological daughter she gave up at 18.

Americashire: A Field Guide to a Marriage by Jennifer Richardson. $15.95, 978-1-938314-30-8. A couple's decision about whether or not to have a child plays out against the backdrop of their new home in the English countryside.

www.ingramcontent.com/pod-product-compliance
Lightning Source LLC
Chambersburg PA
CBHW032102140125
20237CB00004B/106